Inner Story

Understand Your Mind
Change Your World

Dr Tim O'Brien

Layout: Gareth Johns Art Direction + Design / EARN

For Bryony, Mairidgh, Rosie, John

Contents

Chapter One   Inner Story   01

Chapter Two   Changing Your Inner Story   25

Chapter Three   Understanding Your Self   38

Chapter Four   Understanding Your Behaviour   55

Chapter Five   Understanding The Flow Of Fear   80

Chapter Six   Being More Successful   98

Chapter Seven   Being Happier   124

Chapter Eight   Being More Confident   147

Chapter Nine   Being A Better Leader   172

Chapter Ten   Being A Higher Performing Team   199

Chapter Eleven   Understanding Your Changing Story   224

Chapter One
Inner Story

There are two stories inside your head.

One is about your life.
The other is controlling your life.

The story about your life contains the experiences and events that have happened to you over time. This story is your life story. You are aware of your life story. But there is another story inside your head and it is determining what you think, what you feel and what you do. It is the story that convinces you what sort or person you are and tells you what you can and cannot achieve in life. You are living it when you are awake and living it when you are asleep. You are living it every moment of every day.

That story is your inner story.

I call it your inner story because it begins and exists inside your head. Your mind is busy writing it for you right now. But how aware are you of your inner story?

Serina was unaware that her inner story was enabling her to consistently repeat the same mistakes over and over again. David was unaware that his inner story both created and maintained his lack of confidence. Godwin was unaware that his inner story was increasing rather than eliminating unwanted aspects of anxiety in his life. Leah was unaware that her inner story was keeping her trapped in an abusive relationship. Asunta was unaware that her inner story was causing her to become involved in the cycle of gaining and losing weight. Brett was unaware that his inner story was limiting his success and preventing him from playing for his national team. Once they discovered – and changed – their inner stories they changed their world. Your inner story controls your life but it can also transform your life.

1

Everything you do begins inside your head. When your inner story begins it is invisible. As it is invisible you may not notice it or even be aware of it until you sense a feeling that you do not want, notice a thought that you do not need or find your self in a situation where you want to change your behaviour. You should not be concerned if you do not know your inner story. There are many people who are not aware of it even though it is controlling their life too. All stories have psychological power and your inner story is the most powerful of all. You are about to discover yours. I will show you how your inner story is constructed in your mind so that you can become more conscious of it. This will empower you to take control of your inner story rather than allowing it to take control of you.

Working with Inner Stories

I have been immersed in the inner stories of individuals and teams for decades. I have helped successful people in sport, business and entertainment to be the best they can be in their professional and personal lives. Inner stories do not have to be bad to get better. You can make a change for the better even if you are performing right at the top of your game. In competitive contexts if change needs to happen it usually needs to happen quickly. Knowing and changing your inner story accelerates change because it is the fast way to a better you.

I have worked with people who need or want to make changes. They often want to be happier or more confident or less anxious and fearful or more successful. Some want to be a better leader or to perform better in their professional role. They may want to feel better about who they are and be more accepting of who they are. That is how they express it to me but to make it clear I should say that they all want to feel better about who they *think* they are.

I am a psychologist. In my professional work I have been inside the fascinating minds of fascinating people in a range of fascinating places. I am a psychologist who works in a variety and range of environments and contexts too. Of course understanding each context is important but all human contexts are fundamentally about people. They are about how people's minds construct their reality and create their inner stories. Inner stories are universal –

everybody has one. Being able to change your inner story is universal too. Today you have the opportunity to understand your mind and understand your inner story so that you can make changes too. I will be taking you on a journey to the inside of your head. We will explore the mysteries of your conscious and unconscious mind so that you can understand why you think the way you do, why you feel the way you do, why you behave the way you do and why all of this matters. You will be embarking on a compelling journey into inner space.

What to Expect on Your Journey

Your journey will be a voyage of discovery. It begins today with you exactly as you are but when you reach your preferred destination you will have changed your world. You will know how to be more successful on your terms, more confident – especially at speaking in public – how to become happier, how to be less anxious and fearful and how to perform better. You will know how you can be a better leader and create a higher performing team too. You will understand how to achieve any realistic, demanding and challenging goal that you have set for your self or that others have set for you. You will be able to understand, manage and control your thoughts and feelings so that you will be more resilient and adaptable when encountering adversity, unpredictability and those unexpected challenges that life inevitably brings.

Your journey will enable you to understand your self and your sense of self better than you have ever understood it. You will know how to change your behaviour as well as the behaviour of others. All of this can happen when you understand your mind because the capacity to rise to any challenge exists within your own mind. Your mind is busy creating your reality every second of every day. It is also busy creating your inner story and testing it out as you interact with your world. Knowing what your inner story is and what you can do to change it will help you to change your world for the better.

You just have to know how to do it.

This book is grounded in the real world. I am not going to be suggesting that everyone can live in a utopian paradise where absolutely anything is possible. I want to support you in understanding your mind so that you can change your world. Therefore this book is about you being better than you currently are in whatever matters to you and then, once you have achieved your own personal best, continuing to be even better. It is about you getting to understand your mind, learning more about your self and being more successful in your own personal and professional context.

There will be surprises

You will find many surprises throughout this book. I will be explaining that, despite what we have been told for over one hundred years, there is no such thing as self-esteem. I will show you why believing in self-esteem, and including it in your inner story, will never help you to change things for the better. I will offer a new and different way of thinking that will prevent you from falling into the mental trap that self-esteem creates. I will also show you how removing self-esteem from your inner story and replacing it with a brand new way of seeing your self, the way that I see 'self' and the way that I have helped others to see their self, really can help to change lives. How do I know? I have seen it happen. You can read about it in chapter three.

You will notice that I often ask you to be forgetful. Why would I do that? Because, for example, forgetting about happiness can make you happier and forgetting about your goal can give you a real competitive edge. Active forgetfulness is very powerful. I will also invite you into a world where behaviour bounces in your mind and emotions are constantly on the move. A world where it is possible to ask a beautiful question and find a solution to your challenges in a second and where you can learn how it really is possible to make your wishes come true. A world where non-anger management helps people control their anger and where you can change your own behaviour by doing nothing at all. A world where you do not have one potential that is about all of you but where you have lots of different potentials in different areas of your life.

I will also reveal what every person, no matter who they are, must focus on to increase their chance of success. Along the way you will also receive a free pass to the best theme park in the world. I will take you deep inside your mind so that you can understand what is going on in there. As well as taking you into your mind, I will be extoling the virtues of getting out of your mind. In fact, I will be encouraging you to regularly get out of your mind, but only in a good way of course.

You will examine and explore your inner story and will also be invited into the inner stories of others. These include people who are right at the top, others who are on their way up as well as those who are teetering on the edge. I invite you into many inner stories and almost every inner story that I describe is anonymised. Names used are not the real names of the people concerned. Contexts are altered and remain general rather than specific. You will meet many intriguing characters too. These include a hunter-gatherer who has a celebrity friend, a singing CEO who was not appointed to the role because of song-selection skills, an amphibian in need of a little bit of affection, an outrageously negative hypnotist and a blinking swimmer. You will also get to know a terrified member of an antenatal class, a people-pleaser who finally said "no", the solution-focused owner of a cluttered shop and the type of person who notices that their Positive Thinking seminar is half empty.

There are also inner stories from young children, many of whom are on the margins. We can learn so much from children. It is a pleasure to share their insight, wisdom and stories with you. Of course, you also have an open invitation to my inner story. I am the sort of person who believes that everything is constantly moving, interacting and changing – including your brain, your mind, your emotions, your self and your environment. Everything is emergent within you and around you. You may be surprised by the way in which I write 'your self' instead of writing 'yourself'. I do this deliberately in order to emphasise that you have a relationship with your 'self'. You may also be surprised that there are occasions when I explain the complexities of the mind in one sentence. I do this because there are times when a complexity-made-simple approach has immense benefits. If you have quickly flicked through the book you will have noticed that there are some surprisingly empty spaces. This is deliberate too as these spaces are for you to write in.

I am aware that you may choose to read certain chapters in the order that they will matter to you in your world. Consequently, I have attempted to make the chapters stand alone wherever possible. There are occasions when I do refer you to other chapters or offer reminders when that is necessary. The book also flows if you read each chapter in order. Your inner story is created inside your mind so let's begin to think about what an inner story is and how you can discover yours.

We will do this by exploring the inner story of the most important person in the book – you. We will then move on to a jargon-free exploration of what is really going on in that mysterious mind of yours.

Inner Stories are Everywhere

The resolute woman has her inner story, as does the self-sabotaging man. Every child has an inner story. People who are world-class in their field have one, as do those who are just starting out on their career path. Whenever we relate to each other our inner stories connect and interact. When individuals come together for a purpose they create an inner story. Therefore, every team, group, community, business, school and family all have their own inner stories. Inner stories are the inspiration for, and are present in, all forms of creativity including songs, music, poetry, photography, art, fashion and dance. They are played out in sporting, political and social arenas across the globe. The most common way of becoming aware of an inner story is through conversation. When people talk with us, or when we hear them express their views, they begin to reveal their inner story. The best way to become aware of your inner story is also through a conversation, a structured conversation, with your self. You are about to discover how to do that.

What is an inner story?

An inner story is the story inside your mind that,

Describes the essence of who you are.
Defines what it means to be you.

An inner story is the story that you create about the sort of person that you think you are. It is the story that you test out every day in your interactions with others as well as in those private conversations with your self. It is also the story that you tell to your self before you tell it to others – and the more you tell your self a story the more you become that story. That is why you need to be consciously aware of your inner story. You have to check if it is the right story for you because you do not have to be the sort of person that you think you are. It is part of the human condition and the human tradition to tell stories. Yet, one of the surprising and sometimes concerning discoveries in my professional work is that people are often completely unaware of the story that they are telling themselves that is controlling their life. Your inner story runs deep within your mind and for some people it runs so deep that it remains hidden from their conscious awareness. They may not be aware of what their inner story has been doing to them for years.

You are living a story

An 'inner story' is exactly what it says it is – a story. It is a collection of connected thoughts in your mind that are interwoven to create a narrative about you and what it means to be you. However, an inner story is not just a story that you write and tell. It is also a story that you listen to, act upon and live. As it is your story you can edit it and change it if you want to and whenever you want to. But first of all you need to *know* it so that you can establish whether it is working for you. If you do not know your inner story you can sleepwalk through your life, giving permission for anything at all to happen unchecked inside your mind.

Important Messages

I am going to show you a practical way of discovering your inner story and a fast way of changing it. I will also describe how your inner story influences what you think and feel and how it impacts upon your behaviour. This will enable you to change your inner story to a different and better story for you and for what you want out of your life. Before we do that, here are some important messages.

Keep it real

When you discover your inner story whatever you find is absolutely fine. You are discovering it and unconditionally accepting it exactly as it is now. You are not judging it and nor should you. There is no need to feel concerned about your inner story if the content is not what you want it to be at this moment. It has to be the real story about the real you, exactly as you are right now, recognising and accepting all of your vulnerabilities and contradictions as well as your strengths and capabilities.

No need for perfection

You do not have to strive to be a perfect person when you change your inner story. That is not the goal. That should never be the goal. The best way to make a personal change is to begin with acceptance – accepting who you are. It might be uniquely human not to want to be who we are but people who chase absolute perfection set themselves up to fail. We all have to accept that being the sort of person that we think we are can be a real challenge at times, especially as we live in a world that attempts to seduce us into believing that good enough is never good enough. We currently live in a world where perceived imperfections are photo-shopped and the social pressure to look and to be a certain way can result in people feeling unattractive and uncomfortable not only in their own clothes but also in their own skin. This type of pressure will set off thought and feeling associations that can lead to anxiety and depression. Society creates a context where you are encouraged to be more concerned about who you are perceived to be than who you really are. Socially constructed conformity undermines diversity and individuality, but it does not have to be this way and with a different story it can always be different. It is your inner story – be careful not to hand the authorship over to others.

Small changes make a big difference

Nor do you have to make big changes to your story when you discover it. When you make a change you always have to start from somewhere and it is usually more realistic to take small steps before you begin to take bigger ones. Small changes can make a big difference. Everyone's starting point for challenge and change is different. Even when people feel they are the best at something, or are told that they are the best, they can still be even better and continue to challenge themselves further.

With those messages in mind, let's think about what is going on in your mind that is contributing to writing your inner story.

Your Inner Voice is Your Inner Choice

Have you ever considered why thought bubbles in cartoons have words in them? Have you ever heard someone exclaim, usually as they experience sensory overload, "I can't hear myself think"? These examples offer insight into how we all like to talk to ourselves. There is a self-generated voice inside your mind that helps to create your reality. It is the inner voice that allows you to be conscious of what is happening inside your mind when 'I' begins to have a conversation with 'Me'. There are times when your inner voice appears to be silent, other times it does not have much to say, yet on occasions it just cannot resist the temptation to provide an audible running commentary. It can also revel in a spot of after-the-event appraisal: "Why did I say that?" or "Why did I do that?" and even if you try to ignore it or attempt to turn the volume down it just refuses to go away.

Your inner voice is the voice that allows you to hear your self think. It is an active voice: it can be an actively open and positive voice or it can be actively closed and negative. It is the voice that has been influenced by the significant voices in your life. It is even active when you cannot hear it but once you are silent and still and start to pay attention to inner space you notice that it is always there. How often do you stay silent and listen with intent to what your inner voice is saying? My professional experience has convinced me that we do not pay enough attention to the voice inside our head when it talks to us – either positively or negatively.

We do need to listen because your inner voice can create all sorts of damage and debris or it can open your mind and liberate you to achieve things that you never believed to be possible for you. We make a choice about which inner voice we are willing to believe and the voice that we choose to believe helps us to write our inner story. We all have a relationship with our inner voice and we need it to be the best relationship that we have because the voice inside your mind helps to construct your reality.

Closed and negative

You can listen to and believe the negative voice inside your mind. This is the voice that is desperately keen for you to compare your self to others and allows how others look on the outside to affect how you feel on the inside. Listening to your negative voice is important because engaging with it enables you to disempower what you hear. It is when you choose to believe what your negative voice is telling you that the problems start. I call this voice a closed voice because it closes you down as a person and closes down opportunities for you in your life. It is the voice that loves to see you entangled by negative emotions. Let's consider the damage that making this choice can cause.

This is the voice that focuses on one thing that is going wrong for you and then deceptively convinces you into believing that everything is going wrong for you. When we feel bad about one aspect of our self it is there to tell us that we should feel bad about the whole of our self. It beats us up so that it can put us down. It judges and condemns us and does its best to destroy our feelings of worth. It is the guilt-wrapped shame-injecting voice that constantly reminds us that we have to be perfect or that we do not belong. No matter how successful you are your negative voice is always there, prowling and growling, poised and equipped with something detrimental to say to you when you are off guard.

If you are a high achiever it can attack your confidence and belief too, to the point that it can convince you that you are an impostor and will undoubtedly be exposed as one – it is just a matter of time. "You know you are a fraud and that someone will tap you on the shoulder soon and tell you that you have been found out, don't you?" It also tells you that, in terms of your potentials, where you are now is definitely as far as you can go. Your negative voice can talk you out of changing your world for the better.

Open and positive

You can choose to focus on the open and positive inner voice. The positive voice is an open voice because it is open in accepting who you are and it also opens out new ways of thinking, feeling and being. Let's consider the opportunities that making this choice can create.

It can support you in making a change instead of judging you in order to keep you sticky or stuck. It will also allow you to accept that some things may not be working well for you but help you to notice and pay attention to the other things in your life that are working well for you. What is critical here is that paying attention to your positive voice can remind you that while you feel bad about one aspect of your self this does not mean that you should feel bad about every aspect of your self.

The open and positive inner voice releases you from the perfection trap and empowers you to become accepting of your vulnerabilities. It also helps you to address them if you need to. This voice allows you to be more compassionate to your self and to others. It is always there for you when you experience setbacks and will enable you to be more resilient during those challenging times that life can place in front of you. It will help you to make better connections with your self as well as with others. As your feelings are connected to what you focus on, the open and positive voice can energise and lift you up emotionally too. For example, it can encourage you to be grateful for what you have and what is working well for you, even when some things are not working well for you. Being grateful and expressing your gratitude is one way that your positive voice helps you to affirm what is positive in your life.

I recommend that you welcome this voice into your life each day because your positive voice can help you achieve what you never imagined to be possible. It is the voice that really does enable people to be world-class at what they do. That is how powerful the voice inside your mind is. Your positive voice can talk you into changing your world for the better.

You have a choice about which inner voice is going to be the voice that contributes to your inner story. When you hear your negative voice, acknowledge that it exists but tell it you cannot listen because you are far too busy paying attention to the positive voice. You can make a positive choice now.

How to Find Your Inner Story

With your voice in mind, literally, we now move on to one way of eliciting or unlocking your inner story. In doing so I will ask you to begin to interact with this book in a different way from this point. You will need something to write with, as engaging with the book differently from this point will increase its power, purpose and meaning for you.

What sort of person are you?

I would like you to complete the same sentence but with three different responses. Please write your responses in the space provided so that you can look at them, evaluate them and come back to them later if you want to. Here are the three sentences that I would like you to complete. Please be honest.

I am the sort of person who...

I am the sort of person who...

I am the sort of person who...

Please take time to look at these three statements that you have just written. Did you write three positive sentences to describe your self as a person? Did you mix it up and write about you at your best and you at your worst? Did you describe your behaviour or did you refer to what you think or feel? Did you identify what you stand for? Did you describe how you think others see you?

I have asked you to complete these statements because one of the ways that the interwoven strands in our inner story can start to become visible is by describing the 'sort of person' that we think we are. Listen out for this type of phrase, you will notice how often people use it or versions of it:

"I am the kind of person who..."
"I am the type of person who..."

You may have been able to complete the statements quickly, or you may have found that you needed some time to think about exactly what you should write. You may have noticed that feedback from others, such as your parents or friends, has played a part in shaping your inner story. You can revisit these statements any time to think about them differently, tweak them, change them completely or remove them and add new statements. Clearly, there are far more than three strands to your inner story.

What does it mean to be you?

Let's imagine that for one of your statements you wrote, "*I am the sort of person who... would like to be more confident*". This statement provides you with your view of the essence of who you think you are: a person who would like to be more confident. It is a description of what it *is* to be you, it might indicate what it *feels* like to be you but what is important is that it does not define what it *means* to be you. If you are the sort of person who would like to be more confident then what does it mean to be you? For example, does it mean being more confident in terms of how you behave in certain social situations or does it mean being more confident in what you attempt and do not attempt to achieve or does it mean being more confident in terms of how you feel about your self? You cannot understand the impact of your inner story on your world by simply describing the sort of person that you think you are. You also have to define what it means to be you.

Someone once came to speak with me after a presentation that I had given about the mind and performance. He said, "I am the sort of person who is developing a millionaire's mindset". Let's put to one side whether a millionaire's mindset exists and notice instead how such a statement really has no meaning attached to it. It is a description that does not explain what it means to be that sort of person. Descriptive statements about who you think you are do not give you any information that will help you to create current or new ways of thinking, feeling or behaving. Therefore, it is possible that you may think you are the sort of person who

13

is developing a 'millionaire's mindset' but you could find that you are progressively getting further into debt because you have been spending money on attending very expensive courses on how to gain a millionaire's mindset. This is what was happening to the man that I was in conversation with. His mind was busy telling him that he was developing a millionaire's mindset but his bank account was providing real world feedback that suggested otherwise. If you think that you are the sort of person who has a millionaire's mindset you have to know what it means to be you so that you can direct your behaviour towards increasing your wealth. I mention this to highlight that the next stage of the process is to open out your inner story further by identifying what being the sort of person that you think you are actually means for you.

To do this, you have to add something extra to your 'I am the sort of person who' statement. You need to add "and this means...". In the example given earlier you might write, "*I am the sort of person who* would like to be more confident *and this means* that I avoid situations that take me out of my comfort zone, such as public speaking". If that is the case for you, help is on hand in chapter eight.

Please complete the three statements again but this time I would like you to include what it means to be you.

I am the sort of person who...

And this means...

I am the sort of person who...

And this means...

I am the sort of person who...

And this means...

Again, please take time to look at what you have written. 'What does it mean to be me?' is a question that your mind regularly asks. It tests out the answer as you interact with your world. You may be consciously aware of doing this but you also need to be aware that this is happening at an unconscious level too. We will return to the what-does-it-mean-to-be-me question in more detail later when we meet Katie, Cameron and Ezra but now we need to dive deep into the mysterious workings of your mind to find out what is really going on in there.

What is Going on Inside Your Head?

At this very moment your brain is scanning, processing and interpreting sensory information so that it can create your reality and make meaning that is completely unique to you. Split-second after split-second millions upon millions of pieces of information are competing with each other to get your brain to pay attention to them,

> "Pay attention to me, I'm a member of your family."
> "Pay attention to me, I'm a sight that you don't often see."
> "Pay attention to me, I'm a feeling of anxiety."

But you cannot pay attention to everything. With so much to be processed your brain is always deciding what to select and reveal to you and what to reject and hide from you. Your brain is mapping your world at an incomprehensible speed and by fast mapping sensory information your brain individualises your world. This is how your brain creates your mind. Therefore, your mind is constantly changing as your brain makes meaning out of what you are sensing and experiencing as you interact with your world. The way that your brain creates your mind is a uniquely personal process that makes you different from every other person on the planet.

I would like you to imagine that you are sitting in a room with four people. One begins to speak directly to you and you pay full attention to her. Then the second person begins to talk directly to you and you try to pay full attention to him. It becomes difficult to pay attention in this situation, as you cannot process exactly what both people are saying to you as they compete for your full attention. Now imagine what it would be like if a third and fourth person joined in and began talking directly to you, also demanding your full attention. I know from having asked people to participate in this activity that they begin to feel rapidly overwhelmed and overloaded unless they decide to delete or filter out some of the noise and make a choice about what they will pay full attention to. Now imagine what it would be like if millions of people began speaking directly to you. In effect, this is what is happening to your brain as every stimulus that is available to be processed competes for its attention. It is impossible to pay attention to everything. Your attention has to be selective and when your attention is being selective it is also being non-selective; you are focused on some things and not on others. All information cannot be equal.

Searching for patterns

Right at this very moment your brain is selecting what to reveal to you so that you pay attention to it. Your brain is also selecting what to hide from you so that you do not focus on it. It is helpful to think of this process as *patterning*.

Your brain searches for patterns so that it is able to make personalised meaning out of the world as you sense it. My brain is doing the same too. We may both experience the same event but the process of patterning can cause us to experience it differently because your brain tells you what part of reality you should pay attention to and my brain tells me what part of reality I should pay attention to. You might be completely aware of the chilling breeze as it cuts into your chapped cheeks. I might notice that it is windy.

We may both be paying attention to light shining through a window onto the surface of a table. Your brain might reveal the shaft of light to you and then reveal how the colour of the table changes at the very spot where the light hits it. In the same situation my brain might reveal the particles of dust that are dancing together within the shaft of light. The dust was there when you looked but you did not notice or pay attention to it. The colour change was there when I looked but I did not notice or pay attention to it in the way that you did. You will also be aware of the patterning effect if you have ever talked to someone after a sports event that you were both present at and felt that, from their description of what happened, they were watching a different game to you. Patterning is not always accurate. Your brain is busy patterning and responding to experiences that are real as well as patterning and responding to experiences that you imagine. When you are confused, fearful or feeling a lack of control you become far more suggestible. Your brain will search for patterns more intensely in these situations and sometimes sees patterns and connections where they do not exist. We see the world as it is but we also see the world as it is not. If patterning did not occur, your brain would be a hostage to unpredictability and confusion. To prevent this from happening, your brain does its best to establish the relationships between what you sense and what it means. Think about this statement:

"There are twice as many eyebrows in the world than there are people."

Your brain processes concepts such as 'twice as many', 'eyebrows', 'in', 'the world' and 'people'. It then makes meaning out of what I have said so that you can understand it. You will reflect on what I have said and may accept it at face value, literally, or you may question how accurate the statement is. A similar process would occur if I told you that my teeth are itching.

Your brain also patterns by making associations with what has happened in the past to help you to make sense of what you are encountering in the present. It is constantly making associations and generating questions to discover patterns, even when you are not aware of it doing so.

Think of it as if your brain is engaged in a constant conversation with your world. It will generate questions to establish what things are and why they are significant to you.

Questions like,

> What is this?
> Where have I seen something similar before?
> What does it mean to me now?

This is how what is initially presented to your brain as meaningless is given a personalised meaning. Your brain is always searching for patterns and by doing so creates unique frameworks of reference for you. This is how the unfamiliar becomes more familiar, the uncertain becomes more certain and the ambiguous becomes less ambiguous. Patterning is happening inside your head now and, like most people, you are probably unaware of it – but if I give you a hammer you will start to notice nails everywhere.

Creating Your Conscious and Unconscious Mind

How the mind is created is a mystery to many people. How the conscious and unconscious mind is created is an even deeper mystery. I am now entering treacherous and contentious territory, as I am about to oversimplify a spectacularly complex mental process – a process that is made even more complex due to the reciprocal mind-body relationship and the conscious-unconscious relationship. I am also aware that it is a process that some would argue is beyond explanation. Some people would even propose that it is not possible to describe this process at all and any attempt to do so instantly limits complete as well as new understandings of what is really taking place inside your head. However, in the spirit of keeping things simple and practical I am going to reduce this process and describe it in two sentences.

What your brain reveals to you and what you are currently aware of forms the content of your *conscious mind.*

What your brain hides from you and what you are currently unaware of forms the content of your *unconscious mind.*

Your brain hides much more from you than it reveals to you.

Therefore the unconscious aspects of your mind are most of your mind. That is worth reflecting on for a moment because it is very important information to know when you want to change your world for the better.

You pay full attention to certain aspects of your environment and less attention to others. Similarly, you pay full attention to certain aspects of who you think you are and pay less attention to other aspects of who you think you are. Attention shifts and drifts. You might tell your self that you are the sort of person who would like to be more confident but you may not be paying attention to various examples of when you do behave confidently so that you can learn from those examples. Consequently, confident feelings might become tucked away in your unconscious mind.

Your unconscious mind is spectacularly complex and it is also spectacularly powerful. Recently I noticed a silk scarf that had been left on a seat behind me as my train arrived into Paris. Hundreds of people had left the train and were walking along the platform toward the exit. I asked the few remaining passengers who had been sitting nearby if they knew what the person who had been sitting on the seat looked like so that I could return the scarf to him or her. They did not know. Suddenly, I recalled seeing a woman in a grey coat that had a tartan collar. She had been sitting on that particular seat and staring, through her reflection, out of the window. I rushed through the crowd searching for the coat and saw a woman carrying it and returned her scarf to her. Clearly, I had taken a momentary glance behind me at some point on the journey but I was unaware that I had paid attention and taken information in about the people who were sitting behind me. I had done so at an unconscious level. I shall be considering the nature of the unconscious mind in more detail at various points throughout your inner story journey, especially in relation to self-confidence, understanding how fear flows in your mind and in how your unconcious mind can help you become more successful.

Everyone is patterning and perceiving the world differently and it is impossible for anyone to experience your thoughts and feelings first hand. Conscious experience is subjective and qualitative in nature. Only you can know what it means to be you and only you can know how you experience the world. You are like a snowflake, a fingerprint or a mandala. You are unique. Even though we like to say "I know exactly how you feel" to each other, nobody can know exactly how you feel.

Starting to Unravel

Gaining more insight into what is happening inside your head takes us to the next stage as we begin to unravel the strands of your inner story. To do this you begin to pay more attention to what it is you are thinking or feeling or doing. I want to clarify that by using thinking, feeling and doing in that order I am not suggesting that you have a thought, the thought creates a feeling and then you behave accordingly. I do not see such a simple link or straight-line sequence happening in the mind. The relationship between thinking, feeling and doing is complex because they interact with each other and can do so in many different ways. A feeling can affect a thought, an action can affect a feeling and a thought can affect an action. I am emphasising the value of being mindful of your thoughts, feelings and behaviour.

Here are some examples of questions that people have posed to me when they are reflecting on their thoughts, feelings and behaviour. I provide these questions to encourage you to rummage around inside your head so that you can decide what needs to change for you in relation to your thinking, feeling or behaviour. All of these questions start with,

"What is it that I am thinking, feeling or doing that…"

Makes me feel like I don't belong? Makes me think that my life is going nowhere at the moment? Makes me so lacking in body confidence? Prevents me from becoming the best I can possibly be at what I do? Makes me feel painfully self-conscious when I meet people for the first time? Makes me feel so helpless? Makes me avoid the type of conversations that might result in confrontation?

Identify your "what is it?" questions as they will help you to take a fresh gaze at your world and will allow you to focus on what you can think, feel or do different or differently.

Now let's return to why 'what it means to be me' is such an important aspect of your inner story.

A *different and better story*

I was having a meal with Katie. She was overwhelmed by the menu and unable to make a decision. I remember being thankful that she worked in a media business and was not an air traffic controller. I was not talking with Katie about her inner story but she began to reveal it. "I am the sort of person who believes that it is important to be honest. Being honest is really important to me", she followed this with "...and this means that whilst people respect my honesty, there are times when I'm aware that I can appear to be insensitive or rude".

Cameron is an ambitious and determined man. When I first met him he told me, "I am the sort of person who believes you should never say never". Ironically, for a person who believes he should 'never say never', he was managing to say "never" not only twice in one sentence but twice in three words. Cameron holds a leadership position in a global retail business. When he was talking about his inner story he explained, "I am the sort of person who, although I am a senior leader, loves to have fun at work. We spend so much of our life at work, and having fun and being playful is really important to me". Rather poignantly, he added, "...and this means that I have recently started to worry that people might see me as a clown rather than a joker".

Ezra was undergoing her third phase of chemotherapy. Her inner story begins like this, "I am the sort of person who throughout my life has remained positive and strong". It continues "...and this means that I have to remain positive and strong during this very difficult time for me".

Ezra has been unwell for some time. She lives alone and her support network is more medical than it is social. She described how she struggled with her emotions especially when it was just her alone with her mind. She was feeling angry and distressed, wanting to tell everyone how she hated what was happening to her. She saw all of this as being "weak" and "negative" in her situation, the opposite of the sort of person that she thinks she is. Her inner story was not working for her. It was preventing her from being able to see that what she was thinking and feeling was not weak and negative, it was perfectly normal and natural.

Can you see how Ezra's inner story was placing her under pressure and causing her to deny her authentic thoughts and feelings? Her inner story, about always being strong, was compounded by a culturally transmitted belief that people in her position should be positive at all times. This was adding to her stress levels. Inside her mind Ezra was fighting with her self rather than being kinder to her self and acknowledging, accepting and embracing her true feelings. We all have relationships with our feelings and in this situation Ezra needed to have a more compassionate one.

What to do if your inner story is not working for you

These are examples of people who had a strand of their inner story that did not work for them, but what do you do if you are in a situation where your inner story appears to be working against you rather than working for you? The answer is simple – change it. It is that simple, it is that fast and it works.

Remember, you do not have to be who you think you are. Your inner story is a story that is constructed in your mind. It is your story and all that you have to do is give your self permission to change it. If you feel that you have handed the authorship of your inner story over to others then now is the time to reclaim it. You can change your story to a different and better story.

You may be thinking, "how do I change my inner story?" Yet again, the answer is simple and the process is fast. Think of an aspect of you, or a situation that matters to you, where you would like to be different and better. Ask your self what you are thinking, feeling or doing in that situation that needs to change. You do not only have to look inwards, you can look outwards too. You can look outwards at your personal or professional environment and see what needs to change there. It might also be helpful to look at what already works well for others in similar situations to you because all or some of what works for them might also work for you.

In the following chapters I will describe strands of inner stories that work in a wide range of personal, professional and social situations. These include inner stories for being happier, more successful, more confident, performing better and being less fearful. I will describe the inner stories of others too. I do this with the intention of supporting you in understanding your self and helping you to change what you think, feel and do. I also do this because understanding the world of others can offer insights into your own world.

In chapter two I will be inviting you into the world of three people who changed their inner stories – someone in the middle, someone at the top and someone on the edge. For reasons that will become apparent, I would be grateful if you move onto the next chapter quickly.

The Short Story

Your inner story describes the essence of who you think you are and defines what it means to be you.

You are living your inner story when you are awake and when you are asleep.

You tell your inner story to your self before you tell it to others.

Your inner story controls your life but it can also transform your life.

Your brain processes millions of pieces of information every moment of every day.

The unconscious aspects of your mind are most of your mind.

Inner stories do not have to be bad to get better.

You make a choice about your inner voice.

You are the storyteller. You can tell a different and better story.

If I give you a hammer you will notice nails everywhere.

Chapter Two
Changing Your Inner Story

The beauty of your inner story is that it exists in your mind. You are the storyteller and you have the power to change it to a different and better story for you.

In this chapter I will, amongst other things, show you what type of counselling is doomed to failure, encourage you to keep your mind open, suggest that you might not want to be loyal and will show you that you can change your mind in a second. I will also be raising a concern about your potential reaction to young children who are having a tantrum. You will gain an insight into exactly how a change of inner story enabled an Olympic legend to achieve an extraordinary and historic feat and the chapter closes with insight and wisdom from the mind of a seven-year-old girl.

Now that you are clear about what will be happening, and as I want you to find the fast way to being the best you can be, we do not have any time to waste. So, let's move on.

The Fast World

One critique of the world we live in is that everybody wants everything instantly, right here, right now and even sooner if possible. This speed-the-world-up movement originally resulted in the creation of concepts such as fast food. It has now created fast language. Speeding up your language is easy: just combine two words into one and, in an instant, you have saved the substantial time and effort involved in having to say both of them. The need to make a guess or an estimate has become redundant because you can now make a 'guesstimate'. You no longer need to chill or relax – you can 'chillax'. If you want to enjoy camping – but without the unbearable discomfort and questionable rural hygiene – there's a more glamorous version available to you. Yes, you have permission to chillax now because you have guesstimated correctly, it is called 'glamping'. If you would like to learn more about fast language I am sure there will be a webinar somewhere that can help you.

The faster world has also spawned concepts such as 'speed networking' and 'speed dating'. As a consequence of our insatiable need for speed I am now seriously considering launching my latest entrepreneurial idea: 'speed counselling'. Here is a description of how it works. Obviously the client pays their fee up front before she or he enters my consultation room.

"Good morning Tim."
"Good morning, how can I help you?"
"I'm having problems with my husband."
"Leave him and find someone else. Next client please."

As you can see, speed is not the solution to every challenge and nor does speed always equate to progress. There are psychological responses to traumatic incidents and mental health issues that require deeper, slower and intensified inner story exploration. They also require lengthier periods for inner story transformation to begin to take place too. However, in many contexts, changing your inner story does not have to be a slow process at all.

The fast way to a better you
A change to your inner story is the fast way to a better you. It will have an immediate impact upon you becoming the sort of person you want to be and you achieving what you want to achieve. Changing your inner story will change your world. Changing your inner story is as easy as changing your mind. That is because this is exactly what you are doing when you change your inner story: you are literally changing your mind. Some people are proud that they do not change their mind. They like to be, or be seen as, the sort of person who is consistent in how they think and behave. If this develops into a rigid and inflexible thinking style it can lead to stubbornness and cause difficulties in their personal relationships. It also makes them extremely susceptible to certain types of sales techniques. There is no advantage in remaining consistent in your thinking and behaviour if things are not working for you or if you are emotionally stuck. You can change your mind in a second if you

want to. You really can. This is important information because a small change of your inner story can have a huge impact on your life.

Despite what you may have been told, the process of change is not always psychologically challenging. There is no need to feel anxious about change either; you can feel optimistic about it and respond creatively to it because change is always happening. Think about it like this,

Are you the same today as you were yesterday?
Are you the same this year as you were last year?

If you find these questions difficult to answer, try this one,

Are you the same now as you were when you were a one-year-old?

When you were a one-year-old, if you were amongst other one-year-olds and someone started crying you would start bawling and screaming too, even if you were not previously upset. If you were amongst one-year-olds now and behaved in this way it would certainly be a cause for concern and I think it would be a good idea if you booked a few sessions with me. You are always changing. Change is inevitable. Change can and does happen very quickly. You can embrace change.

Change your Inner Story and Change your World

You are always in a position to learn more today, to achieve more today, to be a better person today and to connect with your self and others in a deeper way today. Being better is always possible. Similarly, you are always in a position to have a better relationship with your inner story and to change it to a better story today. We all have inner stories that could work better for us. Let's take Jaya as an example.

Commitment eats loyalty for breakfast

Jaya was talking with me about a decision she needed to make in her professional life,

"Logically, I realise that I have to do it – but I also know that I am not the sort of person who can do it. I am just not that sort of person."

I mention Jaya because you will be able to recognise that whatever it is she feels that she has to do, her inner story is blocking change, holding her back and preventing her from taking action. She is stuck because she is accepting her inner story as being something that is fixed and static. She is also expressing her inner story in a way that many people do: I know the sort of person that I am and therefore I know the sort of person that I am not. Jaya's rationale for her lack of action is that she is not "the sort of person" who behaves in a particular way. So what is Jaya's challenge?

Jaya is a member of a middle management team in a digital media business. She informed me that she had become progressively unhappy over the past two years. Whenever we used to meet we always met in the lounge area of the same hotel. Jaya was always on time. She always sat in the same chair and always drank a particular peppermint tea. If her favoured brand were not available on the day she would never choose a different brand, instead she would choose a different drink. Jaya initially presented as someone who had being 'the sort of person who likes routine' as a strand of her inner story. Of course, like all of us, she might not be what she appears to be. She presented as being quite emotionally contained but within a few minutes of our conversation I imagined that she used to be infectiously enthusiastic. Her inner story had become harmful rather than helpful.

One of the reasons her boss had asked me to work with Jaya was because Jaya was "no longer the type of person she used to be". As you already understand, the language used by her boss here is especially insightful. I began to do what psychologists love to do and used the inside of my mind to access the inside of her mind so that I could explore and analyse what was going on in there. One of the first things that Jaya told me was that she was the sort of person who was "always loyal". I started to investigate. Maybe what initially appeared to be 'routine' as part of her inner story was actually 'loyalty'? After all, she was even loyal to the brand of tea that she drank. My hunch turned out to be right. The value of loyalty, and being a loyal person, had been instilled into her mind by a father who she, somewhat ironically, remembers as being emotionally disloyal for part of her childhood. But he was her father and what her father told her mattered to Jaya. It mattered when she was a child and had clearly shaped her inner story as an adult. Inside her mind loyalty had generalised.

Although her job was making her feel increasingly more "flat and detached" and days when she felt positive were vastly outweighed by days that she did not, she believed that it would be disloyal to leave. Being loyal was causing Jaya to remain in a job even though it made her unhappy to do so. One issue that I have with loyalty is that it can become a psychological prison and this was the case for Jaya. She explained to me that her boss had taken a chance on her and believed in her by promoting Jaya within the business. Jaya thought of herself as the sort of person who is always loyal and who could never be disloyal – but you do not have to be who you think you are and nor do you have to think the way that you currently think. What if Jaya thought about loyalty in a different way?

Relationships that are dependent upon loyalty can become manipulative either consciously or at an unconscious level. Loyalty can have a dark heart. This is because the concept of being loyal contains emotional connotations that create the potential for shadows to lurk within its meaning. We know that abhorrently abusive behaviour has been allowed to run rife within a variety of social and organisational systems where loyalty to senior people is consistently promoted and protected. I prefer the concept of commitment to the concept of loyalty. Commitment is less about restrictive emotion and more about positive behaviour: always giving your best and always being there for others.

What if Jaya was to change her inner story by swapping 'loyalty' for 'commitment'? Then she could say that she is the "sort of person who is always committed" and what a difference that would make to the way that she saw her self and her world. I made this suggestion to her because, mapped against real world evidence, this was a realistic statement for her to make. Jaya had always been committed to her job and always gave her best, even when she was unhappy. Accepting that she had always been committed to her work allowed her to give herself permission to at least consider moving to a new job without feeling guilty. It enabled her to think about being committed and happier elsewhere. It also gave her permission to make a fast change to her inner story. Jaya came to the conclusion that her unhappiness had continued for too long. Sometimes, when things have to change they have to change right now or at some time today. Conversations with her boss ensued and Jaya moved on to a new role in a new business. Changing a word changed her world. Jaya's inner story was keeping her stuck but she had one major thing in her favour – she had agreed to meet with me because she had an open orientation to changing her inner story. If you need to change you have to want to change.

The Value of Openness

If you adopt a more open orientation to changing your inner story you are more likely to pay attention to your open inner voice. If you adopt a closed orientation your closed inner voice will dominate your thoughts, help you to find multiple reasons why you should not change and will keep you stuck. This is why I have urged you not to be judgmental about the content of your inner story. Accept it as it is and then move forward. You can be open-minded and imagine what it would be like if it were different and what that would mean for you. We can all be open to being more adaptable and consequently open to new challenges and opportunities in our lives, even when we feel like we cannot see a way out of a difficulty or when times are really tough. However, your orientation towards changing your inner story can also be closed. This can cause you to be highly defensive of your inner story and remain inflexible in your belief about your ability to change how you think, feel and behave. This will consequently close down many opportunities for you to be different. There are degrees of being closed and there are degrees of being open.

A closed view: addiction

People who have a closed orientation towards changing their inner story always begin by defending it to themselves before they engage in defending it to others. Some will be on their toes, safeguarding it at all costs. It is possible to become so closed and so fiercely defensive that, over a period of time, people are in danger of creating and experiencing psychological and physical isolation. This can eventually lead to shutdown. This process does not happen in every case where someone has a closed orientation but as the degree of closure escalates it can and it does happen.

Addicts will recognise this progressively destructive form of thinking and behaviour. As the process of addiction gets hold of them, and what used to hold them steady in their life no longer does so, they can quickly become defensive when people express views that challenge the way in which they live their inner story. Inside their heads they will search for any piece of evidence, no matter how flimsy or indefensible, that will support their view that they do not have an addiction problem. The shame that many addicts feel about their addiction, dependency, lack of self-restraint and the destructive nature of their behaviour means that emotions are frantically, and at times chaotically, on the move inside their heads. Being defensive can easily turn into being aggressive. Isolation and desolation continues to advance until the addict makes the biggest and most important change in their inner story and becomes the sort of person who reaches out to others to ask for help. If they do not, the consequences can be fatal. Being closed can bring you down but, as you will see, being open can lift you up. Openness as a characteristic is highly valued in many environments. A person's degree of openness is a robust predictor of how well they will perform in any environment that requires creativity and innovative thinking. You can be open in terms of your attitude towards new experiences as well as being open towards understanding your self and others in a new and different way.

An open view: achievement

One balmy summer afternoon Sir Steve Redgrave and I were discussing the psychological processes and strategies that are absolutely critical for consistent elite performance. Steve is a British rower who won gold medals in five consecutive Olympic games over a period of twenty years. In terms of consistent elite performance Steve achieved what no other Olympian had achieved in Olympic history. Steve would like you to know about our conversation.

Steve's inner story is based upon being the sort of person who is driven to compete, and win, by his view that self-belief and determination can help you grasp opportunities and achieve your dreams. This is a description of what it is to be Steve. Now I will explain what it means to be Steve. Having won four gold medals at four different Olympic games and seven gold medals at world championship level Steve decided to retire when he was at the pinnacle of his sport. He had spent sixteen years involved in the physically and psychologically punishing routine of training and competing at the highest level in the world.

Soon after the Atlanta Olympics Steve's future was to change forever. His concerns began when he noticed how dehydrated he was becoming. He was abnormally thirsty and needed to drink large quantities of water after exercise. He decided to speak to a doctor about this. After medical consultations he was diagnosed with Type 2 adult-onset diabetes and bombarded with information about how his life was now going to be different. He was a thirty-five year old Olympic legend who had now discovered that he was going to be insulin-dependent for the rest of his life.

What Steve told me offers an insight into the consequences of having a more open orientation to your inner story as well as a willingness to change your inner story.

Given the situation that Steve was now in, to compete again at an elite level as an international rower would appear to be absolutely impossible. If he had a closed orientation towards his inner story it would have ended something like this,

> " ...and this means that I have now got to live with diabetes and the limiting impact it will inevitably have on my life."

But Steve's inner story, and his orientation towards it, meant that he remained open-minded. He asked many questions including those relating to whether it would be possible for him to come out of retirement and compete to win a gold medal at the following Olympic games in four years time. He recalled one long conversation with his consultant where they explored the possibilities and opportunities that still remained available to Steve. His consultant, although he had no idea how it could actually happen, said that he believed Steve could achieve his dream of competing for another gold medal. Steve decided there and then that with determination and self-belief, plus an illness that was being carefully treated and monitored, he was unable to find a single reason why he should not give everything to compete at the highest level once again.

Steve explained,

> "I decided that diabetes was going to live with me rather than me live with diabetes."

It did.

Steve's openness helped him to change his inner story to incorporate being a diabetic but a diabetic who was going to compete to win at the next Olympic games. The relentless physical and mental training routine was underway again. It lasted for three more years. Pushing himself through the pain barrier was tough enough when he did not have diabetes – now it was so much tougher. Steve competed at the Olympics in Sydney and won his fifth Olympic gold medal.

Admittedly, Steve's achievement is extraordinary. Everyone cannot become an Olympic champion and nor can everyone do so in the circumstances that Steve found himself in – but the process of remaining open towards your inner story and being willing to change it so that you can achieve what you want to achieve is a possibility for everyone. It is always better to have an open orientation towards changing your inner story than a closed one.

The Title of Your Inner Story

I remember explaining the inner story concept to a seven-year-old girl who was experiencing what were described as 'severe emotional and behavioural difficulties' because of traumatic events that had happened in her young life.

In my early career I worked with many children who carried the burden of deficit-labels around with them as they were moved from system to system: emotional difficulties, learning difficulties, behaviour difficulties, social and communication difficulties...the deficit list continues. Sadly, the 'difficulties' label can create thinking that results in children being seen as broken and therefore needing fixing, like a domestic appliance that requires the right expert to locate the problem and carry out the appropriate repair work. The social context for each young person, including the adults that they encounter, is not given enough attention when the label implies that there is a within-child problem. I do not believe that any child needs fixing. Change happens when children who experience emotional needs receive intensified understanding within an environment that is responsive. Intensified understanding requires looking differently. In this context it places a focus on understanding needs rather than fixing difficulties. There are also times when it is not about intervention. Just being there matters: listening, understanding, offering support.

I often used the inner story concept with young children because, amongst other things, it is a workable framework for intensified understanding. It gives them an important message in their time of need: you have an inner story and therefore you can open and write a new chapter today. Importantly, it helps them to understand that what has happened to you in the past does not have to predict your future. How you feel about events and experiences in your past, even if you blame your self for what someone else did to you, does not have to predict your future either.

Kaylee was a resilient young girl. It is worth noting here that the early research about resilience was carried out with children in similar circumstances to Kaylee. It is difficult to learn on your own and it is difficult to be brave and make changes on your own. Kaylee needed support in changing her inner story. In one of my earlier conversations with her I asked her to tell me what sort of person she thought she was. Her response illustrated that this was something she had already given careful private thought to.

> "Do me a favour. Think of most horrible person in the world that you can imagine."

She gave me a generous amount of time in which to think. Once I confirmed to her that I had thought of someone, she continued,

"I am worse than the person you are thinking of. I am worse than the worst person that anyone can think of."

Psychologically, this is a distressing place to be when you are seven years old. Despite her resilience, the meaning that she attached to her inner story was placing her at risk and so we began the process of changing it. During one of our later discussions our conversation came back to the nature of her inner story. She leant forward, one eyebrow raised higher than the other, and enquired,

"Does my inner story have a title?"

What a beautiful question that is. Of course your inner story can have a title if you want it to have a title. It is your story and you can call it whatever you want to. Kaylee was asking because her inner story was changing and she wanted to acknowledge this by giving it a title. Her title illustrated how leaps of progress were taking place inside her mind. It was,

"It's not so bad being me."

She then asked,

"Can my inner story have music to go with it?"

What a beautiful question that is too. Of course it can and Kaylee had already given careful private thought to this too. Kaylee sang the theme tune. Impulsively, yet naturally, we jumped up and down, clapped our hands and danced to it together. It was one of those spontaneous experiences where you turn around and notice a colleague staring at you through the large pane of glass in the door, shaking her head and smiling in recognition of the meaning of the moment.

One element of my work that often remains incomplete is the knowledge of what happens to people once they change their inner story. You touch their lives, their situation improves and everything changes. They move on, or you move on, and you never see each other again. In my mind their life narrative will always remain incomplete just as mine will in theirs. Occasionally I wonder where Kaylee is these days and what the title of her inner story is now. It is a prerequisite that a psychologist has to be comfortable with the ambiguity of not knowing – but there are times when you just cannot help wondering.

Ask your self,

"What is the title of my inner story?"

Now examine the title and see if it is empowering you or holding you back. Reflect specifically on what your world would look like if things were different and better for you, if what you want to change in your life really did begin to change. What would be changing? What would you be doing differently? What feelings would be different? What would you be thinking differently? What would the title of your inner story be now? If you feel adventurous you can also choose the theme tune or the soundtrack to your new inner story too.

Imagining a preferred future in this way provides you with a mental map that can direct you towards what needs to change in your world. The following chapters will help you to navigate the terrain of that map so that you arrive at your desired destination knowing that you are equipped with the psychological skills that enable you to rise to your challenge, whatever that challenge is.

The next stage in understanding and changing your inner story involves understanding your self better than you currently do at the moment and better than you have ever done in your life. It is your chance to discover what it is that really makes you tick.

The Short Story

Changing your inner story is the fast way to a better you.

You are no longer a one-year-old.

You can change your mind in a second.

Be open to new experiences.

Change is always happening. Join in today.

Be committed.

It is better to have an open orientation towards changing your inner story.

It can live with you.

The title of your inner story helps you decide what to change for the better.

You do not have to be who you think you are.

Chapter Three
Understanding Your Self

One of the great mysteries of the mind is how it creates a sense of self. Throughout history, various exceptional male and female thinkers from a range of spiritual, cultural, faith, philosophical and political perspectives have grappled with the concept of what self is and is not. My intention is not to engage in this lofty but important pursuit here. My intention is to help you to think about self in a practical way so that you can work out what it is that really makes you tick. Why? Because some people know more about others than they do about their self and knowing your self is central to changing your world.

In this chapter I will, amongst other things, explain why what has been sold as the solution to being the best you can be will never help you be the best you can be, demonstrate how adding one letter to the end of a word can help you change your world, propose that it is a good idea to see a psychologist if everything is going well and ask you to be far more self-conscious than you currently are. I will also ask you to think about your inner facing and your outer facing self. I am delighted to be able to introduce you to Walker and his world-famous celebrity friend. I need to be very careful about what I say here, because his friend might be your friend too.

Understanding your self in the way that I will be describing in this chapter has helped to make changes in the lives of many people. In some cases these changes have turned out to be transformational.

This chapter will mostly focus on your relationship with your self. It is more about your personal relationship with 'Me' and 'I' than it is about your relationship with other people. By the end of the chapter you will be in a better position to understand what is happening inside your mind. This will help you to understand why you think, feel and behave the way you do. It will also change what you think you are capable of being and becoming. You will notice the connection that exists between emotional wellbeing and self-knowledge.

I would like to offer a definition of self so that we are clear about what the word means when I use it. A definition of self will also allow you to have a better understanding of your self. Self is the sense of 'Me' or 'I' that is created inside your head. You will be used to many concepts that are 'self' related such as self-reliance, self-interest and self-awareness. I assume that, as I mentioned it at the start of the book, you will be expecting me to talk about a different 'self' related topic in this chapter: self-esteem. I shall not disappoint you. I want you to know that,

Self-esteem does not exist.

That may not be much of a surprise to you but I also want you to know that,

Believing in self-esteem will always get in your way
when you want to be the best that you can be. Always.

There is No Such Thing as Self-Esteem

Self-esteem has been a star of stage and screen in the world of psychology for over one hundred years. The self-help, lifestyle and personal development industry overflows with books about self-esteem. If you cannot achieve what you want to achieve, cannot think what you want to think, cannot feel what you want to feel, cannot be what you want to be, then you need to take a good hard look at your self-esteem.

I am pleased to tell you... *You don't.*

The reason put forward for paying attention to self-esteem is that your self-esteem is likely to be low and your personal task is to boost it, build it or raise it – whatever the descriptor is for moving it from low to high. The ability to raise self-esteem is being sold to us as the key to personal success and individual fulfillment.

I am pleased to tell you... *It isn't.*

Self-esteem is not real

I have been deliberately describing self-esteem as if it is real. This is because people talk about self-esteem as if it is real and you would expect me to do that. Now I shall stop. Self-esteem is not real. Self-esteem is not a bridge, it is not a bird, it is not a song and it is not a sandwich. All of those exist, whereas there is no such thing as self-esteem. Self-esteem is an idea, a notion, a concept, or as psychologists like to say, a construct. Far more importantly, it is a mental trap.

Whenever we label something in our world it instantly influences how we think and feel about it. Let's look at the two words that create the label here. There is 'self' and there is 'esteem'.

> Self – my sense of 'Me' or 'I' that is created inside my head.
> Esteem – feelings of worth.

Self-esteem refers to the feelings that you have about your worth as a person: feelings that are created by you inside your mind.

Break Down the Barrier

I know it sounds strange but although it is not real there are those who claim that your self-esteem can be measured. There is no need for you to do the work as there are tests available that can give you the answers. They can tell you what you really need to know: have you got high or low self-esteem? Put another way, do you feel good or bad about who you are as a person? One of the first actions in changing your world is to remove any barriers that prevent you from getting to where you want to be. My view is that focusing on self-esteem creates an insurmountable barrier to being the best that you can be. This is because of the nature of self-esteem. Its nature is hugely problematic.

Here is the problem summed up in a sentence,

> Self-esteem is about all of you as a person.

If your self-esteem is high then you feel good about 'you' as a person – all of you. If your self-esteem is low then you feel bad about 'you' as a person – all of you.

When people struggle to be what they want to be or achieve what they want to achieve they may visit a professional who works in the field of talking therapies. There is a high chance that they could be told, "you have got low self-esteem". I am never sure where people catch it from but because we believe that self-esteem is real, and that it can be high or low, we take it for granted that this assessment must be the truth. Millions of people around the world still buy in to the concept of self-esteem.

But what does "you have got low self-esteem" actually mean? The message could not be clearer: your view of your own worth and your respect for your self as a person is low. This is devastating news. How can such information inspire and motivate any person to change their inner story? How can you find any positives at all in being told that you see your self as worthless?

It is no surprise that being told you have got low self-esteem, and then desperately pursuing higher self-esteem, helps to construct an inner story that can lead to a lack of confidence and reinforce limiting beliefs. It can also contribute to depression.

Another anonymous child

It is not only adults who are presented with bad news about their low self-esteem; shockingly, we do it to our children too and it becomes a limiting strand of their developing inner story. In the early stages of my career I met Georgie who was at serious risk of becoming another one of society's anonymous children. Due to her mother's drug use, Georgie was born a heroin addict. She was still kicking and screaming ten years later. Her aggressive behaviour had caused her to be excluded from mainstream education and kept her poised anxiously on the cusp of becoming another throwaway child within the education system.

Georgie's records from her previous school stated that Georgie had "the lowest self-esteem the school has ever seen". She was experiencing a range of social, emotional and behavioural difficulties and therefore she needed intensified understanding. I needed to understand her perspective on why she was so aggressive towards others as this was the priority issue that needed resolving. By eliciting strands of her inner story I knew that I could support her in making a change. It did not take long to find out. Her reasoning was contained in one answer,

"What do you expect? I've got low self-esteem."

Here we have Georgie absorbing the low expectations that the system instilled within her and articulating the low self-esteem assessment that had regularly been communicated to her. The label rendered her helpless in terms of making a change but helped her to believe that she was the sort of person who could not be different.

Georgie's low self-esteem, her low sense of worth, was also used to validate why she caused difficulties for others. She believed it and so did those who perpetuated it. This is a commonly held view: people with low self-esteem can be actively unkind to others, they are tyrants and bullies in the workplace and they behave in unpleasant ways in their personal relationships because the only way they can lift themselves up is by bringing others down.

The concept of low self-esteem implies a concept of high self-esteem. Therefore, it appears logical to adopt the view that as low self-esteem is bad then high self-esteem must be good. Nobody wants to have low self-esteem; it is far more preferable to have the top-of-the-range version of the construct. It also seems logical to think that being told that you have high self-esteem must have a uniformly positive effect on you and those who interact with you. However, this is not accurate either.

Some people with high self-esteem become the salivating guard-dogs of their ego. They elevate themselves above others and will damage and destroy people to keep their own self-esteem high. Being informed that you have high self-esteem can lead to swashbuckling narcissism and unbridled arrogance: two of the chronic characteristics of no-self-doubt syndrome. The notion that we should strive to have no self-doubt is also problematic. It is helpful to have the occasional healthy dose of self-doubt from time to time. Short-lived self-doubt keeps us grounded and allows us to stay in touch with the negative thoughts in our mind that we have to understand and overcome.

We have a problem here and the problem is not those who are frozen in a state of learned helplessness and nor is it the swashbuckling narcissists.

The problem is self-esteem.

Wave Goodbye to Self-Esteem

Over time self-esteem has become increasingly more taken-for-granted and it still remains unchallenged. I propose that we now have to accept that its usefulness and its lifespan have come to an end. My view is that believing in self-esteem is the pathway to limiting the nature of your hopes, dreams, aspirations and ambitions. It can make you feel that you are a worthless person and restrict your belief in your competence and confidence to achieve demanding goals. But what if you stopped believing in self-esteem? Think about that for a moment. What if you simply refused to allow it to be part of your inner story? What would happen then? I know from my professional experience that you would be psychologically liberated to achieve your potentials. I say that because I have seen it happen to many people, on many occasions and in many contexts.

Self-esteem creates a huge problem. One of the issues with problems is that it is possible to spend hours upon hours talking about a problem and all you have at the end of the discussion is much more information about the problem. Therefore, I will avoid travelling down that particular cul-de-sac and shall now stop describing how problematic self-esteem is. Instead of thinking about it as a problem I will focus on it as a challenge. Many years ago I observed how self-esteem created limitations and dead-ends inside the minds of some of the people I was working with. So I decided to take a journey into my mind, to visit my own inner story and to search for a solution. My solution, a realistic and optimistic solution, is linked to the concept of changing a word so that you can change your world. In this case, a minimal alteration to the word self-esteem can have a maximum impact on your inner story and your life. Just one additional letter is all that it takes.

Today, I would like to introduce you to...

Self-esteems.

Say Hello to Self-Esteems

Decades of real-world experience inform me that people do not have a self-esteem that is high or low. Instead, we have multiple esteems. That's right, lots and lots and lots of them. We interact with others in many personal and professional contexts and we feel differently about who we are and what it means to be us in all of those different contexts.

We also have different esteems that we attach to different areas of our life. For example, we have different esteems relating to the roles that we fulfill. I am Tim O'Brien, father, husband, brother, friend, psychologist, author, musician... the list continues and will be sequenced differently in different situations. Each part of the list has a different esteem, a different feeling of self-worth attached to it. I am not just Tim O'Brien the psychologist. I feel different about my self in different situations. I have different self-esteems. You do too. We all do.

You do not have a self-esteem that is high or low, you have lots of different esteems that vary according to what you are doing and where you are doing it.

It's not about all of you it's about some of you

One of my close friends becomes uncomfortable and anxious when he meets new people; he presents as withdrawn, keeps his distance and is quieter than usual as his anxiety takes time to resolve. If the people who know what he is feeling inside do not encourage him into the conversation he then becomes a socially awkward floor gazer. This is because his esteem is low regarding his ability to create rapport quickly in any new social context. Mundane human activities like getting a haircut is a living nightmare for him because he knows that he will be trapped in a chair and forced to engage in small talk about how busy his day has been or where he is going on holiday. Interestingly, when he is with friends he is often the centre of attention. This is because his esteem is high in relation to how he behaves amongst people that he knows and in situations that are more predictable for him. He does not have self-esteem that is high or low, he has esteem in one context that is low and esteem in another context that is high.

Self-esteem is about all of you as a person.
Self-esteems are about some of you as a person.

Literacy and burglary

I would like to return to when I first started talking about inner stories to children. It was then that I started talking about self-esteems too. I did this to help them understand how they can feel different about themselves in different situations and to ensure that they did not feel bad about their whole self. They usually grasped and understood the concept very quickly. It made sense in their world.

Allow me to introduce you to Clarke, a gravel-voiced apple-cheeked nine-year-old boy whose default assumption was that everyone would instantly dislike him. If it did not happen instantly then he believed it would happen eventually. Like all of us he lived his inner story and tested it out every day, often behaving in a way that would fulfill his prophecy of being disliked. Clarke did not know what to do when he met an adult with a 'come-as-you-are' attitude who did what they could to convince Clarke that he was good to be with. The information that I was given about him was, "this boy's self-esteem is at rock bottom". What do you notice about that statement?

As was usual when I met with Clarke our conversation began with him talking about his dad. I remember Clarke being in a very lively mood at the start of this particular conversation. He described to me how his dad was upset because earlier in the week he had been "caught speeding by a plain-clothes police car". When the conversation turned to how Clarke was getting on at school he behaved differently to how he behaved in school. In the classroom he acted out but when asked to talk about the classroom he acted in. He chose not to make eye contact as he began to tell me how he struggled with the skills of reading, writing and spelling. I explained to him that his skills in school were only part of who he was and asked him about his skills outside of the school environment. At this point he looked at me, became physically animated and his voice rose by an octave. He shuffled on his seat, waved his arms about and began to chirp and bubble. It was like being with a different person. It became clear that outside of school Clarke excelled at two skills: breaking and entering. He was very proud of being exceptional at those skills.

Now let's look at Clarke in relation to his self-esteems,

> His esteem was low in relation to literacy.
> His esteem was high in relation to burglary.

Listening to Clarke describing his out of school escapades, it was clear that Clarke did not have low self-esteem. He had esteems that varied according to what he was doing. In that way, Clarke is just like you and he is just like me. Be aware of being allured into the self-esteem trap because it is a very easy trap to fall into. There are well-intentioned people and books that will seduce you into it. Thinking about areas of your life where you feel good about your self and where you have positive esteems will keep you out of the trap. If there are areas of your life where you feel less good about your self that is nothing to worry about. Remember, just because you feel bad about your self in one aspect of your life it does not mean that you should feel bad about your self in all aspects of your life.

Identify your positive esteems now and identify and include those situations where you feel good about your self. Notice how doing this can make you feel better about your self. You do not have one self-esteem that is about all of you. You have many esteems that are about some of you. Similarly, you do not have one potential that is about all of you, you have many potentials: some of which you will have reached and fulfilled, some you will have travelled beyond and others that are waiting for you to pay attention to them so that they can be fulfilled too.

I feel great – I need to see a psychologist

The world of self-esteem that is high or low, and about all of you as a person, is a world where it would be ludicrous for someone to speak with a psychologist because her or his self-esteem is high.

> "My life is amazing, everything is going well and I feel great about my self. I must make an urgent appointment to see a psychologist."

When was the last time you heard someone say that? However, this is in effect what happens in elite performance environments. A person may already feel great about who they are and what they do, but they are aware that by understanding their mind and raising their esteems a few percent higher – for example in relation to their resilience, composure, belief or confidence – exceptional achievers can optimise their performance. In elite contexts, an extra few percent can make a critical difference, so much so that you can be lifted from first-class to world-class. Understanding what is going on in your mind is not just for those times when life is hard. It does not have to be bad to get better. Everyone can be better at something. In elite environments a person's sense of self can become brittle and vulnerable when performances are below expectations, when outcomes go against them or when they are not selected for a team. This is easy to understand. However, the same can also happen when elite performers are at the top of their game too. Performers are people first; people whose minds are busy creating their inner stories.

For some, being at the top of their game is a scary place to be and can become a psychological burden that is difficult to cope with. Their inner voice can gnaw away at them. Status anxiety can create self-generated pressure and pessimistic projections that will impact negatively upon performance. Being acknowledged as the best, or one of the best, can feel like a lonely psychological space to occupy at times.

Understanding your self enables new ideas, opportunities, contexts, choices and solutions to become available to you. You are in control of the power to make a change. As you journey through this book you will see that actively deciding to forget can be very powerful. Therefore, I will ask you to forget about self-esteem from this moment. You can remove it from your inner story now.

If it works well for you do more of it

You can understand your mind differently when you become aware that the inside of your head is populated with self-esteems. This is uplifting news because it means that you can take a much more realistic audit of what is going on in your life, establish what is working well in some areas and consider what could work better in others. When you have done this you can take a deeper look at the areas of your life where you feel good about your self, where you have positive esteems, and analyse what is working well for you there. If it works well, learn from it and do more of it. If it works well, share it with others. I am not encouraging you to focus on the positives as an end in itself. I am asking you to focus on the positives because when you know what is working well for you it allows you to think about how you can transfer the thoughts, feelings and behaviours from your strength areas where you feel positive to the areas where you feel less positive. Take what works well for you in one area, an area where your esteem is high, and transfer it across to an area where things are not working as well. Please try it. It really does work.

I would be very surprised if you had written the following statement in chapter one – but it is a statement that is always worth keeping in mind.

> "I am the sort of person who does not have one self-esteem that is high or low. This means that I have lots of esteems that can help me be what I want to be and achieve what I want to achieve."

Now that you have thought about self in relation to esteem and esteems let's move on to thinking about self in a different way. I promised that I would introduce you to Walker and to his celebrity friend. That moment has arrived.

Outer Facing Self

I once travelled from coast to coast across the USA on what was rather grandly referred to as a "lecture tour". I met so many memorable characters on my American journey. I also have many wonderful memories. There is one person that I remember particularly well. After one of my presentations an incongruent man meandered towards me. I noticed him amongst the crowd because he was wearing a floral shirt that was so bright he could have worn it in bed and been able to read a book without the lights turned on. His scintillating smile and powerful perfume belied his hunter-gatherer demeanour. He approached me and shook my hand: a greeting of the bone-crunching variety.

The content of our discussion did not stay with me but the unusual way in which he introduced himself did.

"Hi, my name is Walker."

He paused for dramatic effect.

"Tom Cruise – personal friend."

At first I thought this was a socially clumsy attempt to try a basic hypnotic technique: distract the conscious mind so that you are able to access the unconscious mind. He did not use the interrupted handshake, much loved by stage hypnotists, but I still remained on red alert for those two words that would confirm my suspicion: "...aaaaand sleep".

It turned out that this was not Walker's cunning plan at all. We had a short conversation and he disappeared into the distance. Our brief encounter was complete. For deeper reasons only known to Walker, his friendship with Tom Cruise, and I have no idea if it was imaginary or real, was the first thing that he wanted me to know about him. But why would Walker mention Tom Cruise? I was especially interested as it was irrelevant to, and disconnected from, the context and content of my presentation. I assume that it was related to Walker's sense of self. It can be argued that it is your interaction and communication with others that actually helps you to develop a concept of self and this may be relevant here. There are also multiple aspects of self. With Walker in mind, I would like to focus on two of them.

You have a public self – the self that you present to others. By definition your public self is outer facing. When you reflect on your public self you are likely to think about observable aspects of you, such as your appearance and behaviour. You may be concerned about the overall image of you that you present to others when you are conscious of your public self. You are likely to consider whether you make a good impression or not and how people perceive, regard and value you. This is why your public self is often a varnished self. You can think about your public self as being you but with all the lights turned on. Perhaps Walker had worked out the fastest way of presenting his public self to others and Tom Cruise was an intended frame of reference that would impact upon their perception of who Walker was.

As I am sure you can imagine, I spent some time ruminating about what had really happened in my short interaction with Walker. So much so that I almost missed the impatient taxi that attempted to break the sound barrier as it hurtled me towards the venue for my next lecture.

What is your view of your public self?

To what degree do you think your public self shapes your inner story?

In relation to your public self it is important to remember that you create your own reality. You are the writer of your inner story. Your inner story will be influenced by what others say about you and the degree of influence that their words have will depend upon each person. If you completely hand the power over to other people you can experience energy-sapping anxiety because you will always want to be what others want you to be. The desire to be constantly validated by others is a barrier to you becoming comfortable with your sense of public self and being a better you. Inside your mind you will never be comfortable with being who you think you are. If you try to be who others want you to be you will never be good enough.

Inner Facing Self

You have an internal private self too. Your private self is inner facing. Your private self is often an unvarnished self. You can think about your inner facing self as being you but with some or all of the lights turned off. It is the self that only you have access to and only you can know. It is the self that you are in touch with in those quieter private moments and the self that really knows what it feels like to be you. It is the self that knows your secrets too. For some people their private self contains aspects of who they are that they choose not to open the curtains and reveal to others. Some people cannot even peek through the curtains and take a look at who they are because they cannot bear to see what their unvarnished self looks like when the veneer is stripped bare. As your private self is the self that is unobservable to others, when you reflect on it you are more likely to focus on the unobservable aspects of you: your thoughts, your moods and your feelings. Depending on your chosen inner voice, your thoughts can easily become self-judgmental, providing another opportunity for anxiety to become part of your inner story. This is especially so if you are the sort of person who over-thinks and becomes engaged in the type of inner dialogue where 'I' talks to 'Me' about regrets and ever-spiraling negative preoccupations. This will impact upon self-confidence and self-belief.

Returning to Walker, I did not expect him to publicly disclose his private self in our first ever interaction, as that would have been even more unusual than his chosen method of presenting his public self. However, if he did, it might have gone something like this...

"Hi, my name is Walker."

(Pause for dramatic effect)

"This fragrant and fluorescent façade only exists to hide the chilling emptiness that I feel inside."

51

Of course it is wholly unfair on Walker to suggest that he is the guardian of an empty safe – but you get the idea. The concept of a public and private self explains how the self that your mind creates can change from public to private context and vice versa. For example, a comedian can fill a huge arena, connect with thousands of people and make them laugh for hours. Yet, his inner facing self may be in turmoil about his inability to connect one to one with someone to sustain a long-term intimate relationship.

You may know people whose public self presents as gentle and calm yet if you sit next to them when they are driving a car they seem to transform. Aspects of their private self rise rapidly to the surface, as does their superiority bias, and you watch in amazement as they become angry and abusive towards other drivers who, after all, are just random strangers that are momentarily passing though their world. You may also notice that people who present with this type of behaviour often do so with their car windows closed. You do not have to be a psychologist to understand why.

It is impossible to develop and grow as a person unless you have a clear sense of self. It is also impossible to have an authentic inner story unless you have a clear sense of your own self too. To do this you need to reflect on your outer and inner facing self and learn to be comfortable with, and in control of, both. When you have an authentic inner story, a real story about the real you, you can present an authentic self.

This is especially important for people in leadership roles. Firstly, knowing your self enables you to identify the skills that you need to develop so that you can constantly improve your ability to lead. Secondly, and at the risk of stating the obvious, you cannot be a leader unless you have followers. Active rather than passive followership is founded upon the perceptions that followers have about the authenticity of the leader. These perceptions will be based upon, amongst other things, what the leader says and what the leaders does and the connection between the two.

Be Self-Focused not Selfish

By asking you to be more conscious and aware of your sense of self I am not encouraging you to become self-absorbed and nor am I encouraging you to be selfish. I am extoling the virtues of becoming more self-focused. There is an enormous difference between being self-focused and selfish. Being on a plane and, as instructed, putting your life jacket on first so that you are able to help others – that is being self-focused.

Putting your life jacket on first so that you can trample over others and win the race to get to the emergency exit – that is being selfish. The person who is self-focused understands how their self relates to the needs of others, the selfish person only thinks about their own needs. Your awareness of your self has a critical impact upon your confidence as well as your competence. To increase your self-focus, regularly ask non-judgmental reflective questions like,

Why do I think like this?
Why do I behave like this?
Why do I feel like this?
Why do I say those things in those situations?

This helps you to become more conscious of whether your inner story is working for you or against you and provides you with the opportunity to think about what you might do differently and better. Interestingly, these questions also enable you to become more 'self-conscious' – a term that often has negative connotations. I do not use the term in that way. Being conscious of self is a personal quality of some of the greatest female and male leaders across the globe. It enables humility.

Now that you know more about your self, it is time to think about why you behave the way you do. Knowing this will have an instant impact on your ability to change your inner story and change your world. It will also help you to change the world of others.

The Short Story

You do not have one self-esteem that is high or low and about all of you.

You have lots of esteems that are about some of you.

You have lots of potentials.

You have an inner facing and an outer facing self.

You have to be comfortable with both your private and your public self.

We all need a healthy dose of short-lived self-doubt.

It is better to be self-focused than it is to be selfish.

If it works well learn from it and do more of it. Share it too.

When things are going really well for you it is time to book an appointment with a psychologist.

Open the curtains.

Chapter Four
Understanding Your Behaviour

All behaviour is communication.

Your behaviour communicates what is going on inside your mind. It is important to understand human behaviour so that you can be clear about why we all behave the way we do. Once you understand this you can begin to understand your own behaviour so that you can be clear about why you behave the way you do. Knowing this will not only help you to change your behaviour, it will also enable you to understand how to influence and change the behaviour of others.

Understanding behaviour is important if you are a parent – especially if you are a parent of young children – or if you are a teacher. It is relevant in personal and professional relationships. It is also important to understand behaviour if you are in any type of leadership position. When you understand behaviour you can learn how to behave the way that you want to, and need to, in any given situation – which is critical if you work in a performance-based environment or if you are in a situation where changing your behaviour is essential to improving your quality of life.

In this chapter I will, amongst other things, show you how to avoid getting a hug and a kiss from your boss, illustrate how you can change your behaviour by doing nothing at all, explain the four reasons why people behave in a challenging way and suggest where you might want to sit. I will discuss how you can behave better than you feel, prevent you from accidentally hypnotising your self and I shall help you to focus on the behaviour of emotions.

I will describe how I understand behaviour so that I can offer practical advice and strategies that will help you to change your behaviour and the behaviour of others. It might seem strange to you at the moment, but I will also explain how behaviour can bounce. By the end of the chapter you will be the sort of person who not only is able to understand human behaviour better but also understands their own behaviour better.

But first of all, I would like to ask you an unusual question...

Should you sit on the naughty step?

Please allow me to explain why I ask this question. The use of a naughty step offers an insight into what we think behaviour is and how we think behaviour can be changed. The use of a naughty step, or a naughty chair, is a popular time-out technique for managing and changing the behaviour of young children. The intended outcome here is to help a child to learn how to behave in a different and more acceptable manner in relation to the context they are in. The naughty step, much loved by many parenting experts, is an interesting concept as it raises issues about how we understand human behaviour.

The naughty step process goes something like this. Initially a child is told that their behaviour is unacceptable and if they continue to behave unacceptably there will be a consequence. What is important for parents to know, and those who work in a professional setting with children, is that if you use consequences as a method for attempting to change a child's behaviour it is not the severity of the consequence that matters. It really isn't. Your conscious mind enables you to understand what consequences are and once you are told there will be a consequence for your behaviour it will anticipate the consequence on your behalf. Therefore, what actually matters is not the severity of the consequence but that the consequence actually happens.

Even if you are in a situation where you do not know what the consequence will be, buy some time and explain that you are going to decide what consequence is appropriate and explain that it will happen later. If the consequence does not happen then a person's conscious mind begins to set up a predictive pattern and they expect one not to happen in the future, thereby destroying the currency of consequences as a method for changing behaviour. The consequence in this particular context is that the child is taken to the 'naughty step'. Although the next important stage of the process is sometimes omitted, the reason for being told to sit on the naughty step must be explained to the child. This helps them to understand why they have been taken there and what it is about their behaviour that is unacceptable. A brief time limit is set and the child has to remain on the step for that specified amount of time. Once time is up, the parent or carer reminds the child not to behave in a similar way again, expresses love to the child through a hug and a kiss and everyone moves on.

If this time-out technique actually works then why not apply it to adults? After all, many sports have time-out systems for behaviours that contravene the agreed rules. Time-out can be a productive way of providing both a sanction and a cooling off period. Another reason why a time-out system for adults might work is that we all know adults who still behave like children. Don't we? Think about it, after the age of six most children stop sticking their tongue out when they are concentrating but there are still some adults that continue doing so throughout their life.

Cleary there are far more obvious examples that we can observe. There are adults who still struggle to self-regulate; they regress and revert to child-like behaviours until they eventually get what they want. Some do so occasionally when they are stressed others do so regularly as a learned emotional response. You may know adults who stamp their feet or shout and scream in the belief that, because this worked for them as young children, the same outcomes will happen for them now. It is possible that we all know adults who still sulk when things are not going their way. You know, those adults who when they are asked why they are upset remain in an immature psychological space and offer a response such as, "well, if you don't know what's wrong then I'm not going to tell you".

Surely such adults would benefit from a strategy that is aimed at changing the behaviour of children? This brings me neatly to another one of my entrepreneurial ideas: my newly developed product 'Dr Tim's Naughty Step' which I am considering selling to a variety of businesses. I will not be recommending the hugs, kisses and expressions of love from the CEO as that is taking the concept too far. It is also crossing uncomfortable boundaries. However, people could sit on the naughty step at work if they turn up late for meetings, cannot keep to deadlines, if they work in finance and the numbers are going the wrong way, if they are not a starter-finisher or if they are the sort of person who makes a promise they cannot or do not keep. I am sure that you can think of many misdemeanours in your own workplace that would warrant time spent on my naughty step.

The naughty step is in your head
Of course, the idea of adults sitting on a naughty step sounds like nonsense – but why is it that I meet so many adults who do exactly that? They sit on the naughty step inside their head and write their inner story from that perspective. Some were glued to their inner naughty step by their parents many years ago. Sadly, as adults, they still do not know how to set themselves free. They are often unaware that simply giving themselves permission to get off the naughty step will work for them. It really is no more complicated than that. Adults who remain on the naughty step inside their own head are susceptible to self-blaming and self-destruction. They struggle to escape from emotions such as blame, shame, guilt and envy because part of their inner story is written from the viewpoint of sitting on the naughty step. If you have a naughty step as part of your inner story now is your opportunity to remove or demolish it.

Why do you behave the way you do?
When I held senior leadership positions, one of the questions that I enjoyed asking when I was interviewing potential job candidates was, "how can you help us put the 'fun' into dysfunctional?" Not really. I used to ask, "what do you think influences the way that you behave?"

This was a question that people were not prepared for and therefore the answers often presented me with rapid access to strands of the person's inner story including their values, beliefs, motivations and sense of self. That question helped me to see how they made meaning out of their world.

When you strive to be a better you, it is extremely important to think about why you behave the way that you do as this increases the certainty of behaving in a way that will optimise your chance of success. To do this you will want to think about what behaviour is and what it communicates. As a leader, teacher, coach or parent you will also want to understand why some people behave in a challenging way and how you can de-escalate such behaviour. It is helpful if you know that behaviour can bounce and what the implications are when it does start bouncing.

Remember, all behaviour is communication. Your behaviour communicates and expresses, amongst other things, your thoughts, feelings and needs.

What do you think influences the way that you behave? Please write an answer to this question. It will help you to reflect on what you will be reading in the remaining part of this chapter. You can write your answer here:

Behaviour is a matter of perspective and the perspective that you take on behaviour matters. I shall now deal with two common perspectives that appear to explain why we behave the way we do.

My behaviour is inside of me
Here is one way of thinking about why you behave the way that you do and it is one I often encounter when people are dealing with personal and professional challenges and have become stuck. I will call it the *internal* perspective.

Summed up in a sentence,

You behave like you do because it is just the way you are.

This is a perspective on behaviour that sees behaviour as being something internal: your behaviour comes from inside of you. The language that we use offers an insight into how we think. You are able to notice if someone has an internal perspective on behaviour because when they are talking to other people about issues relating to behaviour they will say things such as,

"Do you know what your problem is?"
"He is just like his father."

When talking about their own behaviour they might say,

"I cannot help being like this. This is what I am like."
"This is what I do and its what I have always done."
"I behave like this because I am becoming much more like my
  mum the older that I get."

All of these statements are based on a belief that your behaviour
is determined internally, that you are almost genetically disposed
to behave the way that you do. The concerning thing about the
internal view of behaviour is that it convinces you that your
behaviour is located and locked within you and this raises issues
about what can be done to help you change. Some aspects of the
self-help industry promote this view of behaviour too: if your
behaviour is preventing you from meeting your goals and fulfilling
your potentials then you are the problem and you have to change.
In this case, if something is wrong and requires a quick fix, take
a long, hard and honest look in the mirror. If you are not happy
then it must be to do with you. If you are not confident or full
to the brim with self-belief then the problem must lie within you.
Your environment, your context and your situation are not taken
into consideration.

The internal view does render some people powerless when
trying to change their behaviour. They are their own victims, held
hostage by their own minds. I have met people who really do
believe that they are unable to behave differently because the way
that they are currently behaving is due to their disposition.

My behaviour is outside of me
Here is another way of thinking about your behaviour: I shall call
this the *external* perspective. The perspective taken here is that
your behaviour is not located internally at all. You behave the
way that you do because of the organisations, systems, structures,
processes, communities and cultures that you belong to and that
you exist in.

Summed up in a sentence,

> You behave like you do because factors that are outside of
> you determine the way you behave.

When people adopt this view of behaviour they might argue that
certain groups behave in an anti-social manner because they exist
in a political system that produces low-expectation communities
and a lack of employment opportunities. The external view of
behaviour can be used to explain why people riot and loot on
the streets in certain circumstances. Those who choose to adopt
an external perspective might claim that professional athletes
take performance-enhancing drugs because the system creates
enormous financial rewards for being a winner. They might
propose that in certain businesses some people behave like they do
because they have become brand brainwashed or institutionalised
by corporate systems and practices.

What is worrying about the external view of behaviour is that
individual disposition and difference are not taken into account
at all. The underlying assumptions in the external perspective are
responsible for the proposition that people's behaviour will not
change until the system begins to change. Behaviour is all about
the situation and context that you are in and it is not about you. You
can adopt an internal or an external perspective on behaviour but
do either of these really explain why you behave the way you do?
What do you think?

This is why you behave the way you do

If we adopt the internal or the external perspective then we have
been seduced into an A or B world: human behaviour is understood
as being either internal (A) or external (B).

Polarised A or B thinking is highly problematic. It belongs
in the world of fairy tales: where people are either intelligent or
stupid, either ugly or beautiful and either heroes or villains. Such
thinking dichotomises reality. It oversimplifies reality to create
'either/or' predictability. This type of dichotomania exists in many
different environments. The idea that people are either mentally

weak or mentally strong, that they are either scientific or artistic, is an illusion. In the world of business people are dichotomised as being either creative or commercial or, even worse, either creative or not creative. This is illusory too. Psychologists do not get off lightly here: are you optimistic or pessimistic, rational or emotional, extrovert or introvert? The world is not that simple. People are complex. Context matters. You do not behave the way you do because (A) it is just the way you are or (B) because of the systems you exist in. I believe that your behaviour is not created internally and nor is it created externally. Your behaviour is a consequence of an interaction between many internal and external factors.

Summed up in a sentence,

> Your behaviour is a result of what you bring to an
> environment and what an environment brings to you.

For obvious reasons I shall call my view the *interactive* perspective. This perspective means that you see behaviour as being dependent upon both your disposition and your situation.

Your behaviour is dependent upon a process that involves you and your environment. Every day you bring, amongst other things, your thoughts, ideas, biases, feelings, values, prejudices and beliefs to the environment that you are in. The environment contains, amongst other things, the people and the cultures, communities, structures and systems that you engage with. You do not behave solely based upon, for example, the culture of your workplace. Culture is not something intangible that happens around you affecting the way that you behave. Culture is socially constructed: you interact with it and contribute to it rather than just passively experience it. Every person is a cultural architect: you can legitimise the culture of your team, workplace or community by your own behaviour or you can behave differently and change the culture. In many circumstances culture really does begin with you.

Your behaviour changes according to the context that you are in because your mind affects your environment and your environment affects your mind. Your social environment can have a huge impact on how you think, how you feel and how you behave.

This is why some people behave in a very different way at work than they do at home – in some cases it is almost like seeing a completely different person when you meet this type of colleague outside of the workplace. It is also why changing the variability and unpredictability of adult behaviour can drastically improve the behaviour of children.

The interactive perspective helps to explain why people who appear to be laid-back and relaxed in one situation can suddenly become irritable and aggressive in another. It illuminates why some people can perform outstandingly under one type of leader and lose confidence and belief when they respond to a different leadership style and approach. It helps us to understand why, when people leave their job, it is often not their job that they are leaving – it is their manager or team leader they are leaving. They often move to a similar job elsewhere that allows them to interact with a different leader in a different way. I am conscious too that permanent and temporary medical and physiological factors will also influence how you behave – but even these can be made better or worse by the environment that a person interacts with. The concept of disability is a relevant case in point here. A person's physical disability or their learning disability can be reduced or exacerbated by the environments that they encounter and interact with.

An interactive view of behaviour helps us to make sense of what often happens in schools. A young person dislikes a particular curriculum subject during one academic year and does not perform well in that area. The next year their learning, motivation and behaviour changes and it becomes one of their favourite subjects to study. They will have been fortunate enough to have an inspirational teacher who understands that although the subject content is clearly important, teaching and learning is fundamentally about relationships and making individuals feel that they can learn and achieve. A young person's inner story always changes for the better through interaction with a teacher who makes them feel that they are valued as a learner and as a person.

If you are still not convinced about the interactive perspective consider one more example. If you can drive, try to remember what it was like when you first learned how to drive. Think back to that time now. When you first learned how to drive, the task of driving a car was so challenging that you really had to focus in an intense and structured way on every single tiny detailed aspect of the process of driving. This influenced your behaviour because, for example, when driving you needed a quiet environment to help you to focus on the right thing. Driving and listening to music at the same time would have been absolutely impossible. Now you are able to take a long journey, drive for hours, sing along to music, reach the end of your journey and be so consciously disconnected from the experience that you find it impossible to remember most of what happened along the way.

My proposition is that behaviour is not internally driven. Nor is it externally driven. It is based upon your interaction with your environment. Some people will riot in the street while others with exactly the same opportunity will not. Some people will take performance-enhancing drugs while others with exactly the same opportunity do not. Some people are institutionalised by the business they work in while others in exactly the same situation are not. What you bring to the environment and what the environment brings to you influences how you behave.

You Do Not Have to Be the First to Change

An interactive perspective offers an optimistic view on the possibility of changing behaviour because it demands that you focus on you but also focus on your environment. For example, we know that behaviour can be changed if you provide an environment that is sustained by punishments. Punishment may change a person's behaviour but it is a short-term solution that is often related to a need for command and control. It can also result in the hierarchical abuse of power. Psychologically, punishment does not equip people with the self-regulation skills that enable them to change their behaviour over the long-term. We also know that we can change behaviour by identifying the behaviour that will help the person to change and use the 'catch them being good' method of reinforcement. Here you promote positive behaviour by noticing specific desired behaviours and verbally acknowledging them when you see them – rather than choosing to focus on the behaviour that is undesirable and applying a sanction when you see it. Catching people being good is a more compassionate way of changing behaviour and will provide longer-term change.

When you adopt an interactive view of behaviour you understand that the solutions that you need to enable you to change your behaviour may not be solely inside your head, they can be outside of your head too. This is also another way of changing behaviour. It involves firstly understanding a person's needs and then considering how the environment can change to meet their needs. Instead of trying to change the person you change the environment. This means you can change your own behaviour by you doing nothing at all.

I encourage you to regularly focus on what is happening in your environment because when the environment changes people change. For example, when a parent makes a change to their inner story it can help a child's inner story to change. A change in behaviour from a leader of a team can alter a team member's sense of who they are and what they are capable of doing. We are social beings and we exist in a social context. Your friends and colleagues form part of your environment and they can help you to change your behaviour too. Your social support networks are always a potential catalyst for your own behavioural change. People who I have supported with issues that present as being behaviour related have been surprised by how changing aspects of their social network, or changing their social activity, can change their behaviour. The first point of change does not always have to be the person – it can be the environment.

Challenging Behaviour

One context in which you may want to change the behaviour of others so that you can help them to change their inner story is when their behaviour is difficult to manage, or, as I will describe it here, when they present with 'challenging behaviour'. Sometimes our feelings are so overwhelming that it can be very difficult to behave better than we feel. Behaving better than you feel can be a particular dilemma for toddlers. It is a dilemma for some teenagers and, as described earlier, it is also a dilemma for some adults too.

Challenging behaviour has a function for every person. The function may not be obvious as it can be driven consciously or unconsciously. There are four overarching reasons why people present with behaviour that is challenging. The function of the behaviour might relate to one of these four reasons, but it is also possible that the function of the behaviour could lie in varying combinations of the four. Understanding the function, the drivers of behaviour, can be very helpful when trying to determine the thinking and feeling that underlies the behaviour. It can also be helpful when trying to establish what it is that is happening inside the mind of the person that is reinforcing their behaviour. It helps you to support them in making a change.

I need some attention

People may behave in a way that communicates their need for attention, whatever that attention may look like. For some it does not matter if the attention they receive is positive or negative as long as they are gaining attention of some description. Young children may display challenging and attention-seeking behaviour and on occasions they do not even need to be provoked in order to do so. For example, they can behave in an aggressive way even when they are not angry or emotionally distressed because the function of the behaviour is to gain attention. The function is not to gain revenge or to release their anger or frustration. Attention is usually the assumed reason for certain types of challenging behaviour, in adults and in children, but there are times when attention may not be a factor at all.

Get me out of here

Behaviour might communicate a need to escape from a situation that a person does not want to be in. In this context they may behave in a subtle manner to achieve their goal or, due to their emotional skill set, apply less sophisticated responses to help them achieve the same outcome. Young people who find some aspects of learning difficult may behave in a way that disrupts the learning of others in order to be removed from the classroom by their teacher. Adults who are unhappy in their workplace, rather than make a decision to leave, can behave in a challenging way so that their boss will initiate a discussion about how they can be managed out of the business with a severance payment. The desire to escape from a situation is communicated through a person's behaviour rather than through dialogue.

It feels good

Challenging behaviour may also have a sensory function. There are people who behave in a challenging way because, for them, it just feels good to do so. Their behaviour might communicate a need to be perceived as having power because exercising power makes them feel empowered; it establishes a sense of control. This is especially relevant for people who feel an unrelenting sense of powerlessness as individuals or groups within the systems that they exist in.

Perhaps a less obvious example relates to how self-injurious behaviour can feel good. But this is so. Self-harming can be driven by a sensory need. Although it may be difficult for non self-harmers to understand, in the mind of the person who is involved in self-harming, it can feel empowering – especially at the time that it is happening. It can also feel relieving as physical pain momentarily removes the person's emotional pain.

Give me a reward

Behaviour might communicate a desire for a tangible reward. In some business contexts where bonuses are available for performance outcomes there are people who will behave in a particular way so that they can achieve their bonus. I will leave aside the entitlement culture that offering bonuses can create and highlight instead how the potential of being given a bonus can result in determined, collaborative and team-focused behaviour. It can also result in behaviour that is manipulative and undermining.

The young child screaming in the back seat of the car may not be doing so for the attention of their parents. The child may have learned that if they persistently scream they will eventually get their favourite toy to play with or a favourite sweet to eat because their parents cannot bear the noise and need it to stop. In this way the child learns that challenging behaviour can be rewarded.

A person's challenging behaviour may be challenging for others to manage but it is worth keeping in mind that the behaviour may also be challenging for the person to manage too. We cannot assume that the function of any behaviour is always consciously driven.

Where Do You Sit?

Now that you have thought about why we behave the way we do, let's return to the considerations at the opening of this chapter: should you, or your children, ever sit on the naughty step? What do you think?

I say no because by now you will have noticed that the naughty step reinforces an internal perspective of behaviour. If you think about the message that a child processes when they are taken to the naughty step you can see how it promotes an internal view. The received message inside their mind is "I am naughty. My parents even have a special step on the stairs that is for naughty children just like me". Remember, children have an inner story too and "I am the sort of person who is naughty" has serious implications for a child's developing perception of self.

What options other than the naughty step are there? How might you de-escalate challenging behaviour? I would like to suggest three options that are easy to apply.

Errorless choices

When I worked with children and young people whose behaviour was challenging and was at risk of going out of control I used to say to them as they headed towards a crisis, "you are now in a situation where you have two choices". I would then offer two choices, both of which were errorless choices, offering the person a way out of the difficult situation that they were in. Whatever the chosen option it was always an errorless decision. The temptation in these situations is for the adult to offer a moral dilemma to the child – one choice that is a good choice that will help matters to improve and another that is a bad choice that will escalate the situation further. This response is based on the adult's inner story and not on the child's needs. Errorless choices will also work when you are dealing with the challenging behaviour of a team member if you are a team leader in an adult environment.

It is so easy to be impulsively revved up by the surge of energy and intensity that exists in situations where behaviour is escalating towards a crisis point. Learning how to control your mind prevents this from happening. It is also vital to be focused on what is happening inside the mind of the person who is reaching crisis point. Some emotions will be racing around on their own mental Grand Prix circuit while others are twitching in desperation to get behind the wheel. With such high-speed emotional chaos going on in their mind the person will struggle to find a rational way out of a difficulty. This is where you step in and find one for them. There is an important issue here about what reality you focus on in order to help to de-escalate a situation that could become increasingly more challenging. Although your eyes may convince you that you are dealing with the behaviour of the person, their behaviour is just an outward presentation, an expression, of their emotions. What you are actually dealing with is the behaviour of emotions.

Naturally we tend to deal with the behaviour that is before our eyes and forget that we are really dealing with the behaviour that our eyes cannot see – the behaviour of emotions inside someone's mind. This is not easy to do because emotions are tricky to deal with. When someone is angry their emotions constantly duck and dive, they hide behind each other and then reappear, they gather together and regroup and they lock themselves onto particular thoughts so that they can do everything in their power to destroy or minimise your intervention. Anger is not a pure emotion. This is why angry people often need non-anger management, but I will leave that discussion until chapter seven. What makes the situation more complex when people are angry is that there will also be emotions that are searching for a resolution but they will have been forced into the background. When you are dealing with challenging behaviour you have to locate those emotions and empower them. Errorless choices help you to do exactly that.

Errorless choices help the person to feel that they are learning how to self-regulate as well as learning how to make sense of their confusing emotions and control their own behaviour. If you are offering support and preventing the situation from becoming too explosive and colourful, there is great value in staying calm and patient and modelling calmness and patience. In sport, calmness and patience always make it possible to achieve a positive result in the final few seconds of a game. The same applies when dealing with challenging behaviour.

When someone is recovering from being on the verge of an emotional and behavioural crisis the initial trigger emotions in their mind remain on the move and refuse to go away, even when the situation appears to have calmed down. You have to remember not to send out an invitation to them for at least fifteen minutes after a serious behavioural incident. Give the person some water too, that always helps.

The power of because
Another option is to ensure that you use the word 'because' when you are asking people to change their behaviour. I recommend,

"I want you to... *because...*"

If you work in environments where you encounter people who are presenting with challenging behaviour change can happen quickly if you respectfully explain what you want them to do rather than what you want them to stop doing. I always use 'please' and 'thank you' because they are key de-escalation words. These words indicate that you are not threatening and nor are you a threat. Having explained what you want the person to do, follow this by using the word 'because' as this is another key de-escalation word. When you have used 'because' provide the reason for wanting them to do what you are requesting and expecting. You want the person's brain to pattern for what they can do differently to improve the situation rather than causing their brain to focus on what they are doing now which needs to stop. Focus on the right thing.

'Because' is an incredibly powerful word. When you use it you alter the patterning in someone's brain. Some people, when they hear the word 'because', will pay full attention to the reason that you provide for asking them to change what they are currently doing. As you know, your brain is patterning so much information that it does not pay attention to everything. This creates the potential for people to hear 'because' and not to listen or pay full attention to the reason that you give but to move straight on to acting upon your request. When you use the word 'because' you always create the possibility that people will process the structure of what you are saying more than the content. By this I mean that their thinking process will work in the following way, "she is now asking me to do something. Here comes the reason why". Even though they might not pay attention to the reason given, they may still do what is requested.

We are often naively optimistic about how intently others listen to us. Some people hear 'because' and they do not pay full attention to what comes after the word as they assume that a rational reason is on its way. People become more suggestible to what you are asking them to do when you use the word 'because'. Try it out, ethically of course, *because* it works.

Time to think

You may put forward the argument that the naughty step will change the behaviour of some children. I agree with you. It will. However, the change is based on a psychological theory that can teach pigeons to dance and dogs to jump through hoops. There is a distinct lack of reflection involved in such contexts and this brings me to my third option. If you want long-term meaningful change you will gain more success if you ask a child to take time-out to think about their behaviour and how they might change it. This is because thinking about your behaviour is critical to changing your inner story so that you believe that you are the sort of person who can regulate your behaviour. One way of helping someone to do this is to separate the person from their behaviour when you discuss issues that are directly related to behaviour. As a parent you might say to a child,

"I love you, but I do not like that behaviour."

At work you might say,

"I respect you but this behaviour is unacceptable and cannot continue. Your behaviour has to change."

This does not make the person feel bad about who they are and prevents them from becoming involved in the spiraling decline of believing that their behaviour is locked inside them and they cannot change. When you are dealing with people whose behaviour is challenging respect the person and reject the behaviour.

If you have been siting on the naughty step inside your own head then give your self permission to get off it today. If you were excited about going to your manager or boss tomorrow to suggest the introduction of a naughty step for people to sit on at work then I am sorry to dampen your enthusiasm and spirit.

Instead you could initiate a thinking step. This could be a special place where a leader or a colleague can ask people to go to so that the person can sit and think about their behaviour, how their behaviour impacts on themselves and others and why it needs to change. They could think about the role that the environment plays in their behaviour too. When they have finished thinking they could reflect on what they are going to do differently next time. Now that really would make a difference.

Behaviour can Bounce

Now we move onto one of the mysteries of the mind that is so mysterious that it can appear to be completely baffling. I was in a large store recently. As I was using my card to pay for the items that I had purchased I saw a notice on the counter next to the payment device. It was in capital letters and assertively insisted,

"Do not leave your card in the machine."

I asked why this notice had been placed there and was informed that the store was becoming concerned about the increasing amount of distracted customers who had left their bank cards behind after paying for their goods. This resulted in staff spending too much time dealing with phone calls about lost cards. I asked how successful this notice had been in terms of making sure people remembered to take their card with them. I was told that the strategy had been unsuccessful. In fact, it had made the situation worse. Rather than reducing the amount of cards that had been left behind, more people were leaving their cards in the machine than before the notice was put in place. I was not surprised. Are you?

I was walking through the bustling streets of a city when I saw a man collapse onto the pavement. He appeared to be hyperventilating. As I ran over to him I noticed a woman kneeling down at his level. She spoke in a hushed voice that was comforting and reassuring,

"You will be OK – do not panic."

Obviously, these supportive words were intended to keep the distressed man calm and to prevent anxiety from escalating and fear from flowing. The problem was the advice did not appear to be helping. I was not surprised. Are you? Fortunately a passing paramedic appeared on the scene like an urban super-hero and was there to intervene with immediate success.

Last week someone opened a recently created file on a screen so that I could add some content to it. She said to me,

"We have not backed up the file yet. Whatever you do – don't delete it."

My attention was immediately drawn towards the delete icon. I have to be honest and say that I was impulsively and somewhat childishly tempted to press the delete icon just to see what would happen and how she would react. I will stop asking you if you are surprised.

When I was speaking at a conference I asked the audience to close their eyes. I did this to entice them into a state where they could concentrate on their thinking. People often close their eyes when they think because it eliminates patterning and allows them to look inwards. We had been talking about the mind and so this did not seem like an unusual request. I asked the audience to listen carefully to what I was about to say, allowed a period of silence to occur and said,

"Do not think of a red ball."

They smiled. Some laughed because they were doing exactly what I was asking them not to do, they were thinking of a red ball.

Pause and think for a moment; what is really happening in all of these situations that I have just described? Have you noticed yet? To help you notice I would like to make you aware of a process that I refer to as 'bounceback'. Knowing about bounceback and keeping it out of your inner story is another fast way to change your world and to change the world of others. I would like to explain why.

Don't Think About Bounceback Now

Bounceback can occur when someone structures a sentence that contains an instruction – but – they begin the sentence with *'do not'* or *'don't'*.

"Do not panic" may cause you to panic because "panic" is the last word that you hear.

"Don't delete it" may have caused me to think about deleting the file, as "delete it" are the last words that I heard.

Now you can see why I was not surprised that more people were leaving their cards in the machine.

Those who understand unconscious processes know that behaviour can bounce back in your mind. For example, whether they work in a clinical, therapeutic or entertainment setting, hypnotists know exactly how to use bounceback to their benefit. The process that occurs when a hypnotist starts to guide you into a relaxed state is known as hypnotic induction. During the process of induction a hypnotist needs you to become increasingly more responsive to their words as that is, in effect, what you are expecting to happen when you agree to participate. They are not taking away your free will and nor are they taking control of your mind. They are using language to internalise your attention, making you less likely to resist and more likely to be suggestible.

They may well use a carefully planned script to guide you into a deepening state of internally focused relaxation and altered perception but to you, and to your conscious mind, this hypnotic induction may seem normal and natural in that context. Even if the induction feels like it is naturally conversational, you will have no conscious sense that it may have been prepared and structured beforehand with meticulous precision. Early in the induction the hypnotist may say something like,

> "...and as you become aware that you are breathing slower, do not think about relaxing deeply. You are so sleepily comfortable that you do not notice how your eyelids feel so much heavier now."

Superficially this seems quite straightforward but if you focus more carefully on the language that is being deliberately used, you will see how bounceback works. I will add italics for illustrative purposes as you look again at what she said,

> "...and as you become aware that you are breathing slower, do not *think about relaxing deeply*. You are so sleepily comfortable that you do not *notice how your eyelids feel so much heavier now*."

The italics emphasise how the hypnotist is using a form of negative or indirect suggestion. She is telling her client what he should not do in order to activate the behaviour that she wants from him. Paradoxically, she is telling him what he should not do so that he will do it. She is causing her client's behaviour to bounce inside his mind. Bounceback helps the hypnotic process to get underway.

Why does bounceback happen?
It really does seem baffling as to why we can respond to what we are being told not to do by actually doing it. My view is that this is possibly due to it being a direct response to patterning. Remember

that as your brain is creating your mind it is processing your world at an incomprehensible speed and has to select what information to reveal to you and what to hide from you. "Do not" or "don't" at the start of a sentence creates a specific type of ambiguity that your brain has to fast-map and make split-second meaning from.

What is happening? What do these words mean?
Where have I heard this linguistic structure before?
What should I do now?

Your brain is always searching for information that will direct your behaviour. "Do not" is not a noun. "Do not" is also not a verb but you will have noticed that "do not" is often followed by a verb. This type of ambiguity can cause your brain to quickly hide the words "do not" and reveal the other words as if they form the beginning of the sentence. That is my explanation of this puzzling and intriguing process. In the hypnosis example "do not" is hidden from you at an unconscious level and "think about relaxing deeply" is processed consciously. Similarly, at a later point "notice how your eyelids feel so much heavier now" is processed at a conscious level to encourage you to focus on your heavy eyelids. This hypnotist really does know her stuff because adding the word "now" at the end of the sentence increases the possibility of the words she is saying being processed as an instruction.

Bounceback can have more serious implications too. For many years in the UK the government has run a campaign in the media that is aimed at stopping people from driving their vehicles when they have been drinking alcohol. The slogan for this campaign is "Don't drink and drive". If those who designed the campaign knew more about bounceback they would have created a radically different slogan. They could have had more success with other slogans too, such as, "Don't drive tired", "Don't use your phone when driving" and "Do not speed". What do you think they could have used as their slogans instead?

Bounceback in sport
Why does structuring your sentences so carefully, especially when you are giving instructions, matter so much? Well, for someone to

stop paying full attention, even for one second, can be a problem in many contexts. I am sure that you can think of many examples where this applies. I would like to use sport as an example but you can apply what you read here to a wide range of contexts.

If you are involved in sport I am sure you have heard people in leadership roles shouting, "don't lose focus". I also know that people say these exact words inside their own head during competitive sport. In chapter six I will explain how you never lose focus, but for now I shall use this "don't lose focus" example so that you can see how language has a direct consequence upon the way that your brain patterns. The last two words you process in this example are "lose focus" and this increases the chance that your brain will search for information, such as inner thoughts and feelings, that indicate that you are starting to lose focus and lock them into your mind. The implications for behaviour in a sporting context are clear. So what do you say instead?

You can prevent bounceback by rephrasing the intentions of "don't lose focus" in a more positive way. This is a skill that you can learn. Instead of saying "don't lose focus" say, "stay focused".

When times are tough, instead of saying, "do not give up" and offering your brain opportunities to search for physical and psychological evidence that you are about to give up – rephrase it positively and say, "stay strong ".

Help your brain to help you
If you are leading a team, or in a team, remember that a team is a community of mind and think about what is going on in every person's mind within the team. Anyone in a leadership role should be conscious of bounceback when communicating information to a team. When giving tactical instructions make sure the instructions speak clearly to the conscious mind of each team member. Tell them what they should do rather than what they should not do. Always communicate what you want people to achieve rather than what you want them to avoid.

Once you are aware of bounceback you become attuned to noticing it in various situations. Here are three examples:

"Do not forget to..."
"Don't make the same mistake again."
"Don't worry about it."

When you hear language that can create bounceback take it as an opportunity, inside your mind, to practice restating what you hear in a positive way, in a what-to-do rather than what-to-avoid way. How would you restate those three phrases positively? You might say,

"Remember to..."
"Do something different next time."
"Be positive about it."

You can see the impact that the language you use has upon your own behaviour as well as the behaviour of others. Always give instructions in positive language; this increases your repertoire of positive responses. It will keep your mind focused on expecting to achieve what you want to achieve. If you expect it to happen you allow it to happen.

Awareness of how your behaviour can bounce back can provide you with a competitive edge psychologically, especially when you need to keep your thinking clear in high pressure situations so that you get the performance behaviours you want personally and from a team. If you talk to your self, or others, and use language that can create bounceback, catch your self doing it and re-phrase what you are saying in a positive way. You can do the same when the words of others can cause behaviour to bounce back in your mind.

Finally, I have an extremely important message that I would like you to pay full attention to:

Don't tell everyone you know to buy this book now.

The Short Story

All behaviour is communication.

You can change your behaviour by doing nothing at all.

The thinking step is better than the naughty step.

Your behaviour is not locked inside you.

Focus on the behaviour of emotions.

You can respect a person and reject their behaviour.

There are four reasons why people behave in a challenging way.

Behaviour can bounce back.

Environments and people can change for the better.

Your behaviour is a result of what you bring to an environment and what an environment brings to you.

Chapter Five
Understanding The Flow of Fear

Emotions do not stand still. They are always on the move and fear is probably the quickest out of the starting blocks. But fear is more than an emotion – fear is also a process. It is no slouch as a process either. Controlling fear as an emotion is a challenge for many people but controlling fear as a process is something that every person can do.

Now that you have a better understanding of your inner story, your sense of self and why you behave the way you do, let's focus on the essence of that speedy and slippery emotion that prevents people from changing their inner story and being happier, more successful, more confident and excelling in whatever they do. Handling fear and really getting a grip on it may seem to be more challenging than juggling with wet fish – but it really is possible to do it, especially when you catch fear as it begins to move inside your mind.

This chapter is not about fear avoidance and nor will I be telling you that going eyeball-to-eyeball with fear will help you to overcome every single fear that you have. My aim is to help you to be mindful of fear and to understand it as a process as well as an emotion. I want to encourage you to understand and engage with how fear flows within your own mind so that you can interrupt and control it.

This chapter will help you to be the sort of person who can disempower fear and regulate it so that every time you potentially face it again you will have the insight, skills and energy to combat and control it. Interrupting the flow of fear is important because when fear begins to flow rational thinking gets washed away in the torrent.

In this chapter I will, amongst other things, describe some of the potential dangers of antenatal classes, highlight the benefit of singing "Happy Birthday" at a business meeting, suggest that what you think you are frightened of may not be what you are frightened of, describe how you should respond to an amphibian in need and explain what to do if you turn up to your Positive Thinking seminar and it is half empty.

Your Relationship with Fear

Everyone has a relationship with fear. When offered the opportunity to change their inner story many people want to be better at dealing with fear or overcoming fear. Most people recognise fear as an emotion and how it sabotages their thinking, hijacks their feelings and dominates their behaviour. "I cannot go into that room because there is a spider in there", "you will never get me on a plane because I know it will crash". These are two statements that describe two different relationships with fear. Before we delve deeper into the nature of fear and how fear flows I would like you to consider your own relationship with fear by answering the following question.

What frightens you?

Please answer this question by writing complete sentences rather than a list of words. There is a reason for asking you to write full sentences. You can write your answer here:

It is likely that when answering this question in sentence form you will have written,

"I am frightened *of*..."

I have not used a psychological technique to prime you to begin your sentence in that way. It is just that we naturally talk about being frightened of things because this is the way that most of us frame fear inside our minds.

"I am frightened of heights, success, thunderstorms, germs, balloons, enclosed spaces, the unknown, crowded areas, time on my own, failure, clowns, injections, dentists..."

How we describe fear shines a light on the nature of fear. You experience the fear of something because you have attached fear to that something. This statement may seem self-evident, however, it is very important information when it comes to understanding fear and preventing it from flowing in your mind. We attach the emotion of fear to something and we then learn to become frightened of it. Fear only exists because you give it permission to do so when you attach it to something. This provides the possibility that you are frightened of fear as a process and an emotion rather than being frightened of the object or experience that you are attaching fear to.

Fight, flight, freeze or flock?
Fear is an emotion that I have met in many contexts in which I have worked. Although fear generally gets a bad press it does have a biological upside. Fear provokes the behaviours that are required when we begin to experience different categories of threat and, as psychologists like to say, when we feel we are no longer 'the locus of control'. In situations where we judge that safety and security are under severe threat the brain triggers two rapid-reflex choices: stay or go. Stay and defend your self or do your self a favour and get out of there as quickly as possible. This instinctual survival response is referred to as 'fight or flight'.

In some contexts the feelings we attach to the fear of something are so completely overwhelming that a person becomes paralysed by fear and just cannot take any action at all. This is where the third reflex option arises: the 'freeze' response. Your brain does offer another option, known as the 'flock' response. This can happen when a person in a group is unsure what to do and simply follows the decision made by the majority of the group: a type of safety-in-numbers or herd-mentality response. It is important to note that you can learn these responses to fear. The good news is that if you can learn them, it also means that you are able to unlearn them and learn new responses instead.

Kiss a Frog Today and Every Day

Many people are held back and inhibited by fear because fear creates learned emotional responses that develop into habits, routines and ruminations that are difficult to control, interrupt and break. These unhelpful and at times debilitating responses are driven by thoughts and feelings that you do not need and do not want. These are the thoughts and feelings that hold you back and prevent you from taking a leap of faith – faith in your self – and then simply seeing where you land. When you take a leap of faith you may not land where you want to but your world will have changed in some way because when you land you will be in a different place to where you started. You may find that new answers or new options are open to you because you took the leap. You may just be proud of having taken the leap. Of course, you might also land where you aimed for. As princesses in fairy tales know, there are times when you have to take a leap of faith and kiss a frog.

Your thoughts and feelings are driven by the content of your inner story, which can allow fear to flow until it becomes so pervasive that you can attach fear to fear. In the same way that some people are anxious about being anxious, there are people who are frightened of being frightened. Often, they are not aware of it.

When you are frightened of being frightened you can become stuck in one way of seeing and knowing. You steer clear of taking a fresh gaze at a situation because what you are likely to unearth could be frightening to you. This keeps you stuck. In this context, being stuck means that you never have to step out of your comfort zone and therefore never get close to experiencing the flow of fear. If that is the case for you, then trust your self and just go ahead and take a leap of faith – kiss a frog and see what happens.

In fairy tales frogs are reviled because they symbolise baseness, threat and evil. What is interesting is that the princess knows this but she is willing to see beyond the visual presentation and the feelings that are racing around inside her mind. This is the point at which she takes a leap of faith and kisses the frog. She can only hope that the outcome will be the one that she desires. She might succeed or she might fail but that does not prevent her from kissing the frog. Kiss a frog today and every day.

Some people will not take a leap of faith because they attach fear to failure. The fear of failure can be terrifying for them. Some are so frightened of failure that their preference is to stand still. They can be skilled in providing justification for remaining passive. Others who fear failure might attempt a challenge but will do so in an over-cautious and risk-averse way. This is a means of protecting their sense of self from the emotional implications of failure. They may think that they are frightened of failing but they may not be. They might be frightened of what people will say about them if they do fail. Fear builds all sorts of hurdles and barriers inside your mind.

The Flow of Fear
The causes of fear are highly individual but it is not causation that I will be focusing on here. I shall focus on the experience of fear because most people experience fear in similar ways. They experience fear as a process. Fear flows physically as well as psychologically. When it flows in your mind you can also feel it flowing in your body. One moment you can feel it in your stomach making you feel nauseous and a few seconds later it will have moved and you can feel it in your chest affecting your breathing.

Are you frightened of what you think you are frightened of?
Rather than consider what contexts cause people to be fearful, such as fear of darkness or fear of the unknown, I would like you to think about the process of how fear moves inside your mind. Knowing how this happens will help you to recognise how fear flows for you and to take action to interrupt it and control it. It also helps you to understand that, because fear flows, what you think you are frightened of may not be what you are frightened of. In chapter six I will describe how people who think they are frightened of failure may not fear failure at all. I will also provide you with many suggestions about what the fear of failure might really be the fear of. For now, let's think more about the principle that what you are frightened of may not be what you are frightened of.

Have a happier Christmas
I was once asked if I would get in contact with Paula. It was early

December and Christmas time was bringing a specific form of annual domestic stress for Paula's family. Paula's daughter Izzy was frightened of beads. Izzy is six years old. She had been frightened of beads for some years and the flow of fear had generalised inside her mind so that she was now frightened of anything that resembled beads including baubles, marbles and small round sweets. Nobody was able to enter Paula's house if they were wearing beaded jewellery due to the obvious distress it caused for Izzy.

Christmas had become a difficult time because they could not have baubles hanging on the family Christmas tree in Izzy's house and certain other decorations frightened Izzy too. Whenever Izzy saw beads or anything that looked like beads she instinctively fast-tracked to the freeze response. This would happen at home, at school and in public places such as the local shopping mall. As soon as she saw a bead she would stand still, scream and shake until the beads were removed from the person. If that did not happen quickly enough then Izzy would be removed from the beads. Paula wanted to speak with me because she was unsure what else she could do to help her daughter. Accommodating Izzy's fears seemed to have made matters much worse and it was becoming stressful for everyone in the family, including Izzy herself. Paula felt that it might be time to try another option and to challenge Izzy's fears instead.

Why would someone be frightened of beads? This is a rational question but difficult to answer because the flow of fear extends beyond the parameters of rationality.

Why would someone attach fear to beads? This is a much better question because it allows you to empathise with the person concerned and to consider what it must be like to be in their world. It also invites you to consider the possibility that what someone appears to be frightened of may not be what they are really frightened of.

I began to wonder. If Izzy had an intuitive freeze response to seeing beads then perhaps there was a fundamental issue of survival and security occurring here? Maybe Izzy saw beads as a threat to her? This was worth exploring further. Could it be possible that Izzy was fearful of swallowing a bead and choking? I asked Paula if Izzy had ever swallowed a bead. No, she had not.

Never. I continued to rummage. I asked if Izzy had any problems related to swallowing? Paula paused for thought and told me that Izzy did have an operation a few years ago because she had a reflux issue that made her start to choke when she was swallowing her food. Now we were getting somewhere. Can you see where?

Maybe, what Izzy appeared to be frightened of was not what she was really frightened of? If Izzy was not frightened of beads maybe she was frightened of choking and dying? I asked to speak with Izzy. Having asked her lots of non bead-related questions I approached the issue of her attachment of fear to beads. She told me that beads were scary. I wanted to calibrate how scary they were in her world and so I asked her what was the worst thing that could happen if she saw a bead. She told me that a bead could, "if it wanted to", choose to jump from a necklace and fly around the room. If she was in the room when that happened she believed that it would find her, fly straight into her mouth, stop her from breathing and kill her. She felt the same about all other bead-like objects. Even if she turned away from them she believed they could still fly around the room and find her. This is a distressing scenario for a young mind to cope with and must have felt like a waking nightmare.

Izzy was not frightened of beads. My hunch was right; she was frightened of choking and dying, a fear that was likely to have developed before she had an operation. It seems that fear continued to flow after her operation because although physiological repair had happened psychological repair had not. Remember, all children have their own inner story that is created inside their mind. Fear had continued to flow and had projected itself so that it became attached to beads. I was able to suggest an intervention that would enable Izzy to change her inner story and interrupt the flow of fear. Paula and Izzy set about the work involved. Life at home began to improve and everyone had a happier Christmas.

This may seem to be quite an unusual story to you but many principles remain the same throughout all cases where fear flows. What you think you are frightened of might not be what you are really frightened of. Also, the evidence that you collect from your world may be false. You have to think about what is really happening. Beads do not have a will of their own but if you believe they do then the possibility of them jumping down your throat becomes not only real but also terrifying. Fear flows in mysterious ways. Fear behaves like a gas that is determined to fill any space it can find in your mind so that you will eventually become overwhelmed and suffocated by it. Those who are close to you may feel your fear too.

I would like to tell you two stories that you may be more able to identify with. In these stories, both about the flow of fear, you will notice fear as a fluid process and a behaviour-influencing emotion. With their permission, I would like to invite you inside the minds of Mike and Jon.

A thought that arrived with its own shadow

Mike is well known in the media. He is an incisively witty and erudite man who, incidentally, believes that there are two types of people in the world: radiators and drains. Mike once attended an antenatal class. I say 'once' because the experience was so traumatic for him that he never returned despite becoming a father on two more occasions.

At the start of this Sunday evening suburban antenatal class the mums-to-be were asked by the group leader to sit in a circle. This became the inner circle. She asked the dads-to-be to sit directly behind their partners thus creating an outer circle. The group leader began the first whole group activity of the evening by insisting that being pregnant is such a life changing experience that, "it is completely normal to feel worried about having a baby".

The presupposition here is that it is completely abnormal if you are not feeling worried. This is just the type of thought that sends a party invitation to feelings associated with neurotic and anticipatory anxiety and encourages fear to flow, as you are about to discover. If you were a member of the group and arrived to the class not feeling anxious this introduction enabled you to become anxious about not being anxious. The course leader also emphasised that it was important to "share all of our anxieties with each other". Clearly, anxieties are like babies – better out than in.

With her introduction to the activity complete, a caring sharing experience began. The women were first to share: one at a time, clockwise around the circle. Mike was feeling excited about having his first baby but he made sure that he still paid respectful and careful attention to the women as they spoke about their anxieties and concerns. The course leader concluded their contributions, "Thanks for sharing ladies. Guys, it's your turn now. Around the circle we go".

She pointed to the first man as an indicator that he should speak. He began to talk of being anxious about seeing his partner in the pain of childbirth. Unfortunately for his partner he was anxious about how he would deal with it. The second man articulated a more practical concern about finding time to decorate the baby's bedroom. By the time the third man was speaking Mike had noticed that he was going to be not only the last man to speak but also the last person to speak. His heart started to pump faster as he experienced increasing levels of anxiety. Inside Mike's head fear was desperately waiting for the sound of the starting gun. Mike was not concerned about speaking in front of others, he did that for a living, but now he felt that all of the women were looking at him. They really were expectant mums because he thought that they were expecting him to be the person in the group that would say something really funny. You will recognise patterning at work here. Mike could not think of anything amusing to say and as a result became anxious. Neurotic anxiety came to the party and fear began to flow.

He told me,

"At this point it felt like I was losing control of my thinking."

Have you ever felt like that? Are you able to recognise what is happening to Mike?

Mike also noticed that due to the mind and body connection fear flows in your body as well as in your mind. As each man spoke Mike described a knotting in his stomach that moved to his chest. He began to discover that the flow of fear creates confusion too. As pickpockets and stage hypnotists know, when you are confused you become less rational and far more suggestible. His thoughts started to go with the flow. Then, "out of nowhere", a thought came to him. This was a deep disturbing thought. A thought he had never been consciously aware of until this very moment; a thought that arrived with its own shadow. Mike wanted to escape from the room. The content of what the men were sharing had now become noise to him. All that he could focus on was the thought that must never be spoken. No matter how hard he tried to control his thinking, the flow of fear rendered him powerless and the thought refused to go away. It is always difficult to fight against a shadow. Inside his mind he kept repeating to himself, almost in time with his heartbeat, "don't say it, don't say it".

You know about bounceback and will understand that this is probably the worst thing he could say to himself at a time like this, especially in a heightened state of suggestibility. His turn to share arrived. At first he did not respond. Then, impulsively, he announced,

> "I am frightened that I am going to die before my son
> is born."

Mike described how the whole group turned their heads to stare at him. Now the silence itself became pregnant. It was broken when his wife turned to him and shouted, "What? You've never told me that before." He responded,

> "Of course I haven't told you that before. I have absolutely
> no idea why I said it. It just came out. I honestly don't
> mean it. I have no idea where it came from."

You do.

You know that your brain will search for evidence to support what you think and feel. Mike got caught up in the notion that every woman in the room was expecting him to say something that was hilarious. What happened here is that Mike became focused on evidence that was false but appeared to him to be real. This can occur when fear begins to flow. Remember, patterning is not always accurate and what he thought was happening was not really happening. His mind was playing tricks on him. Fear took its toll by enabling his unconscious mind to present one disturbing thought to him that became the focus of his full attention. As the thought came to his conscious awareness, despite his best efforts, he was unable to keep it to himself.

Tell me more tell me more...

Let's enjoy a visit to a different person's mind and see what you notice about what happened to Jon, the CEO of a business in the UK. Jon is tall, intellectually elegant and physically cumbersome. He informed me of a recent visit to China where he was completing a business deal.

Jon was in a room that was full of Chinese businessmen and businesswomen. He was standing on a stage at the front of the room accompanied by a female colleague from the UK and a local interpreter. The Chinese CEO was speaking in Mandarin into a microphone. Apparently he was informing the group about the completion of the deal. Jon was facing the audience, nodding and smiling as if he understood what was being said even though he did not have a clue. The CEO turned to Jon and reached out towards him. Jon thought they were about to shake hands. Somewhat disturbingly for Jon, instead of a handshake, his Chinese counterpart held the microphone to Jon's mouth and began to whisper into his ear. The interpreter explained to Jon, "It has been a very happy occasion and he would like you to sing a song to everyone please ". Jon explained to me,

> "In that moment my mouth went dry and my mind
> went blank."

Have you ever felt that type of physical and mental shift? Can you recognise what is happening to Jon here?

Jon was not prepared for this request and was hoping that the interpreter was joking. She wasn't. Fear began to flow. Jon looked at the smiling hopeful faces before him and felt "a sense of dread". He was unsure if post-deal singing was a feature of Chinese business culture that he was unaware of. He did not want to upset the gathered group especially as he was their "special guest" from the UK. He remembers a series of connected thoughts,

"I am shy. I don't enjoy giving board presentations never mind standing on a stage in front of so many people in a different country."

"Singing in public is a nightmare for me but I have to sing if they ask me to. They will think I am rude if I refuse to sing."

"I'm a CEO so everyone will be expecting my performance to be really impressive."

As well all know, when a CEO decides to sing we always expect an impressive performance from him or her. Nothing less than impressive will do from a singing CEO. As you can see, fear was flowing and false evidence was influencing Jon's behaviour. Jon could hear the following words resonating inside his head, "think of a song, come on, think of a song". He described to me how, at one point, he even heard himself say that phrase aloud, as did his audience. Then everything began to change. He raised his right leg into the air in a slow and exaggerated fashion. He began to create a loud syncopated beat by bringing his leg back down and banging his right foot on the wooden floor. His legs and hips began to gyrate in an unrelated manner. Unfortunately for all present, including Jon, his thoughts decided to go with the flow and his brain told him to open his mouth. Over-enthusiastically he burst into song...

"Summer lovin' had me a blast.
Summer lovin' happened so fast..."

You can imagine how this excruciating scene became even more hip-thrustingly unacceptable when he reached,

"Well-a, well-a, well-a huh! Tell me more, tell me more...."

The meeting was concluded with a brief and diplomatic round of applause, allowing Jon to rush to his awaiting car. In the privacy of an airport-bound limousine, his female colleague prodded,

> "Jon, what on earth happened there? Why did you sing a
> song from *Grease*?"
> "I honestly don't know. I don't even like that song."
> "Why didn't you sing "Happy Birthday" or "God Save the
> Queen" or something like that?"
> "I don't know. It came from nowhere. It just happened."

When these types of fear-flowing incidents take place people often say, when they reflect back on what occurred, that a feeling or thought "came from nowhere". This is not the case, they always come from somewhere. You know where.

I am sure that you will be able to map what has happened to Mike and Jon onto many situations that people you know have experienced in their personal or professional lives. You may be able to personally connect with the flow of fear that they both experienced. You may even identify with the different stages at which they could have interrupted and regulated the flow of fear.

False Evidence Appearing Real

The flow of fear reduces feelings of control. The flow of fear removes your sense of being present in the moment. It also distracts your attention and increases your suggestibility. All of this highlights how your brain will continue searching for patterns so that it can make sense of your world – even if the patterns it finds are false ones. Therefore, when you are rising to a challenge where you might experience fear, it can be helpful to reflect on the FEAR acronym:

False
Evidence
Appearing
Real

You do not have to be frightened of all spiders. That spider in the room is substantially smaller than you and the evidence suggests that, in the vast majority of cases, it cannot harm you at all. Statistically it is more dangerous to drive a car than to be a passenger on an aircraft. You may be patterning false evidence because of the fact that most car crashes do not appear on the national or international news whereas most plane crashes do.

If you notice that fear is beginning to flow inside your mind, get in touch with it and interrupt the flow by establishing what evidence is false. Ask your self the question that is always worth asking when your emotions are rampant and entangling,

"What is *really* happening here?"

This enables you to pattern for information that will help you to regulate and control what is happening in your mind, focus on the right thing and become the locus of control. When striving to be the best you can be, prepare your brain so that it patterns for the information that helps you to prevent the flow of fear from occurring. Fear can grip you in many different ways. Yet, understanding how fear flows inside your mind helps you to grow, thrive and succeed in the most creative, competitive and demanding environments in the world. There are times when we all have to learn to develop and employ more sophisticated responses to fear. We also have to start somewhere. Reflecting on the meaning of the FEAR acronym and framing fear in this way is a practical and pragmatic starting point.

I have explained how fear makes you suggestible. When fear flows your mind can convince you that if you go to the top of that high building you will be the person that falls off. The flow of fear can convince you that if you tell him that you love him he will think it is too early in the relationship, feel trapped and will work out how to reject you. Inside your mind anxiety is loud but fear is even louder. Fear can make you so suggestible that you believe that you can predict the future. When fear causes you to predict the future it also causes you to fear the future. There is a certain style of thinking that I have encountered in my professional work that adds fuel to this future-fearing and future-predicting fire. It is known as catastrophising.

Why Have a Problem When You Can Have a Catastrophe?

I have met people who are caught in a negative rut because they continually focus on the wrong thing, persist in focusing on the wrong thing and develop negative and destructive thinking styles as a consequence. Catastrophising is an example of one of these styles. Catastrophising includes irrationally imagining the worst possible outcome in any given situation. Put it this way, why have a small problem when you can have an out-of-proportion crisis instead? Catastrophising is the mental equivalent of dropping a stone into a pond: it creates a ripple effect in your mind. What starts as a negative thought begins to ripple outward and the outward momentum is sustained by the presence of crisis generating "what if?" questions. Sometimes "what if" questions stand alone, but they can also become part of a catastrophic sequence inside your mind. "What if I travel to San Francisco and there is an earthquake while I am there...and what if I am hit by falling rubble... and what if that causes me to lose my memory...?"

"What if...?" "What if...?" "What if...?"

When this happens you begin to think in ever increasing circles. You become anxious about the future and fear begins to flow. Instead of focusing on the here and now, your thoughts project into an imagined future, and as the circles get bigger so will the outcomes of your "what if" questions. This is how, inside your mind, you move closer and closer to an imagined catastrophe. Catastrophising does not only apply to imagined experiences, it can also be applied to something negative that has really happened to you – such as losing a game, a relationship break-up or missing out on the job promotion that you wanted. Catastrophising is a thought-leader in convincing you that if you have tried to be the best you can be and have not achieved what you wanted to achieve, it is a catastrophe, you are a failure and you must not try again. As your catastrophising inner voice might say, "if at first you don't succeed, give up".

The Positive Thinking seminar was half empty
For some people catastrophising is not only an occasional way of

thinking, it can become habitual and develop into a way of being. It is also possible to develop a generally negative orientation towards making meaning out of your world. When you have a negative orientation you become the sort of person who will notice that the Positive Thinking seminar you were advised to attend is half empty. It is also unlikely that you will notice that it is half full by the time you are leaving. Having a negative orientation can cause you to miss opportunities in life. It creates stress and invites fear to flow. People with a negative orientation say "yes but..." far more than they ever say "yes and..."

A negative orientation can cause you to predict failure rather than imagine success. If you provide the positive thoughts your brain will search for the light at the end of the tunnel but if you provide the negative thoughts your brain will search for the tunnel at the end of the light.

The uplifting news here is that if you are the sort of person who gives the ripples of negative thinking permission to unsettle you, you can learn to think differently. You can gain a more realistic perspective by actually accepting that you catastrophise, accepting that you have developed a negative orientation. Acceptance of any difficulty releases you from being trapped and controlled by it. When you accept that the way in which you perceive your world needs changing you become more conscious of your thoughts and feelings and can select the right thought and feeling attachments that will allow you to change your world.

The Ripples of Positive Thinking

Changing your world for the better happens faster when you pay attention to the positives more than you do to the negatives. I am not suggesting that you ignore or that you deny negative thoughts, definitely not. Acknowledging and analysing negative thoughts helps you to deal with them and learn from them. The denial of negative thoughts does not stop them from being present in your mind and having a direct influence on your inner story. I am suggesting that when you focus on positive thoughts and listen to the open voice inside your mind you put your self in a position where you can change your inner story to a different and better story.

Positive thoughts can expand and crowd out negative thoughts. You can connect positive thoughts with optimistic feelings. As your thought circles move outwards your brain will collect references of positive and successful experiences and boost your self-belief. This helps you to be more grateful for what you have and to focus on what is working well for you in your life.

Positive thoughts increase life satisfaction and gratitude. Positive thoughts help you to become less anxious. Positive thoughts encourage you to kiss the frog. Positive thoughts enable you to interrupt the flow of fear.

The Short Story

Fear is a process as well as an emotion.

Fear flows psychologically and physically.

When fear flows rational thinking gets washed away in the torrent.

What you think you are frightened of may not be what you are frightened of.

Fear creates learned emotional responses that you are able to unlearn.

You can be frightened of being frightened.

The flow of fear feeds catastrophising.

Positive thoughts can crowd out negative thoughts.

Acceptance of any difficulty will release you from being controlled by it.

Kiss a frog today and every day.

Chapter Six
Being More Successful

Your success is constructed in your mind before it ever happens in real time. Therefore your mind determines how you maximise your chance of being more successful.

In this chapter I will, amongst other things, suggest that you need to be anxious, insist that you forget about your goals, recommend that you might not want to eavesdrop on what people are saying about you and I will also state outright that motivation is not enough to guarantee your success. At times I will refer to elite sport as a context but the content of this chapter does not only apply to sport, it applies to inner story strands for success across a wide range of personal, professional and social situations.

People can fall at the first hurdle when aiming to be more successful because they encounter the fear of failure. I shall describe how to get over that particular hurdle. Most of us would agree that successful people are focused people, so I shall also deal with that elusive concept 'focus', explain what it means and reveal what everyone needs to focus on to increase their chance of being more successful.

Success does not happen in a straight line and becoming more successful is not a smooth process. It is likely to include rough roads, bumpy rides, setbacks, defeats and failures. Therefore, I shall be recommending a particular way of psychologically navigating such a journey so that you can deal with adversity and arrive at your desired destination more resilient than when you started out. As an added bonus, I will help you to learn the fast way to get back to sleep when you wake up in the middle of the night.

You are reading this chapter because you are the sort of person who would like to be more successful in some way and possibly on your terms. You may already be successful in many areas of your life but you already know that inner stories do not have to be bad to get better. Everyone can improve and develop. Everyone can be more successful. You may want to learn how to perform better in a sporting or business setting. You may have set goals that you want to achieve. You may want to be more successful in getting what you want out of your personal life.

The best starting point is to begin by looking at what your current inner story is in relation to being successful and whether it is enabling you or holding you back. You should also identify what success looks like for you. But first of all, let's approach one of the biggest hurdles to changing your inner story.

Fear of Failure

Success implies the possibility of failure just like winning suggests the possibility of losing. Rising to any challenge can create the wrong type of anxiety in your mind when you begin to think about, and focus on, the possibility that you might not achieve the outcome that you want. It is important to remember that what you focus on will expand because people who fear failure find that their confidence begins to wane at the point that thoughts about taking on a challenge emerge from their unconscious to their conscious mind. This causes their conscious mind to visualise negative outcomes and provokes unresolved anxiety around the possibility of failure. Here we have some of the key ingredients for a fear of failure recipe.

Thinking about the possibility of failure can prevent people from imagining success. It reduces their appetite for success and convinces them that they should not make any attempt to be successful. Fear of failure controls your behaviour.

Let's pretend

There are many ways of approaching the fear of failure. One way is to avoid the fear of failure by pretending that failure does not exist. This may sound ridiculous but there are people out there insisting that there is no such thing as failure. The inherent problem with pretending that failure does not exist is that you remove the opportunity for you to experience, analyse, accept and move on stronger from failure. The far greater problem is that failure *does* exist in the real world.

One popular phrase claims, "There is no failure, there is only feedback". Try telling that to a sports team in a changing room when they have just lost a major final or have a go at telling it to an individual who has given absolutely everything over a period of years and has just found out that they have not been selected for their national squad. Try telling it to any person who has worked as hard and prepared as well as they could but has not passed an important examination or to someone who was not chosen for the big part that they auditioned for. Try telling it to someone who has lost out on the dream job that they have always aspired to get. I am not convinced that they would agree with you that there is no such thing as failure. I am convinced they would not take kindly to the suggestion that it does not exist.

Let's get real

I understand that the intention of the phrase is to help people frame failure as being something different and I accept that it is always possible to frame things differently in your mind. However, framing failure as feedback ignores what is happening inside the mind and in the real world. It is similar to people who are anxious being told to distract their mind when they feel anxious instead of paying full attention to their anxiety, understanding and accepting it, and then doing something about it.

If you distract your thoughts when you feel anxious, you might temporarily suppress your feelings but the anxiety still remains, it does not miraculously disappear. You will continue to experience it. When you deny anxiety you feed it. People do experience failure and they process it as such. Even the most heroic of failures will eventually be processed as failure. We have to get real because failure is real and we have to persevere through it. Failure happens. Failure hurts.

Of course, there is an important relationship between failure and feedback: analysing why an outcome did not go as you wanted it to does offer feedback about what can be done better next time. But it is vital not to deny the existence of failure nor the psychological impact it can have on a person or a team. Framing failure as 'feedback' denies you the opportunity to connect with your self and work through your deeper and more painful emotions so that you are better equipped mentally the next time things do not go your way.

Is it really the fear of failure?

Whenever you set out to succeed you inevitably put your self in a position where you can fail. Failure happens and consequently people do fear it happening. Some of us are so frightened of failing that we become passive and never attempt to be a success.

As I have explained in chapter five, what you think you are frightened of is often not what you are really frightened of. We frequently project our fear of one thing onto something different or we allow our fear to flow from one thing to another – but we are usually not conscious of doing so. This means that there are people who think that they are frightened of failure, but they are actually frightened of something else. They may be frightened of letting other people down, taking risk, commitment or the humiliation involved in explaining failure to others. It could be that they might be fearful of being seen as a failure. They may be frightened of being labeled a failure or judged by others as a failure. I have met people who not only fear the judgment of those who matter to them they also fear the judgment of people that they admit to having no respect for. I even know people who fear the judgment of parents that are no longer alive. That is what fear of failure can do to you. It is always possible that the fear of failure could be the fear of something else. It might even be the fear of kissing the frog and succeeding because of what success might mean for someone when they do achieve it. Although it may seem paradoxical, the fear of failure might really be the fear of success. You can pretend that failure does not exist or you can take a more realistic stance and accept that it does.

Failure is an option but so is success

Another way of avoiding fear of failure is to believe that failure is not going to happen to you. Failure may happen to others but you are the sort of person it does not happen to because the word 'failure' is not in your dictionary. I am sure that you will have heard people who are rising to a challenge insist that "failure is not an option".

It is as if this statement has the mystical power to ward off the failure demons. I am always concerned when I hear people use this phrase because, in competitive contexts, failure *is* an option but then again, so is success. If you have the courage to consistently keep pushing your self and attempting to win, you have to accept that there will be times when you lose. In many contexts the end results are there for all to see when failure happens. Failure can be and can feel brutal and unforgiving when the outcomes, outputs and results do not go your way. As a consequence, people who are striving to be more successful accept that failure exists and that failure can happen to them. They learn how to develop psychological strategies that enable them to understand what failure means for them and how they will respond to it should it happen.

Accepting that failure is an option helps people to prepare thoroughly, to stay buoyant and determined in the face of adversity and recover faster when they encounter failure.

You are not a failure
If you experience failure it is important that you are clear that it does not mean that you are a failure. Failure happening to you does not mean that you are the sort of person who is a failure. In a win or lose context, either as an individual or as part of a team, an honest assessment of your performance may result in you acknowledging that you did contribute to you or your team losing but this does not mean you should internalise failure as being about you as a person. When you internalise failure, and attach failure to feelings about self, the structures and the communication systems in your brain that have already tagged and stored previous negative experiences in your life kick into gear. They will automatically alert their own high-speed courier service and send as many previous negative experiences as possible to your conscious mind so that you can be reminded of them and pay attention to them. Sadly, in this situation any chance of showing compassion to your self flies out of the window.

People who internalise failure will eventually open the fridge to eat the chocolate they have been storing away. They do not apply for the leadership role they so desperately want, they never make the first move to speak to the person that they would like to get to know better and they abandon the creative project that mattered so much to them when they began it. Some will compete and perform, unfulfilled, at a level that never takes them out of their own comfort zone. As entrepreneurs and educators know, fundamental to the learning process is being able to understand that failure happening to you does not mean that you are a failure.

Experiencing failure does not mean that your hopes and aspirations should be limited either. Failure does not have to be the plunging step into sunken dreams and shattered hopes. If you want to be more successful you should focus on what you want to achieve rather than what you want to avoid. One thing you want to achieve is to be in an emotional state where you have no fear of failure: a state where the potential for fear of failure has been eliminated from your mind. If you want to confront the fear of failure and remove it from your inner story you have to accept that it does exist and acknowledge that it can happen to you. Accepting that something can happen releases you from being controlled by the fear that it might happen.

Nobody wants to fail but to be more successful you have to be willing to fail. Being willing to fail increases your chance of success. Sometimes your mistakes can contribute to a loss or a failure. Everyone makes mistakes. Failure does offer you feedback, often distressing or uncomfortable feedback, but it is feedback that gives you the opportunity to learn and to do something different and better next time.

Love to Win or Hate to Lose?

Being successful is often associated with being described as 'a winner' and being unsuccessful with being described as 'a loser'. Some people that I have worked with have told me that they love to win more than they hate to lose. Others have told me that they hate to lose more than they love to win. How about you?

I ask because being the sort of person who loves to win or hates to lose offers an insight into your inner story and highlights whether you have the best inner story for maximising your chance of being a success. In chapter one I described the process of how your brain creates your mind: how it reveals information to you so that you can focus on it and hides other information from your conscious attention. Due to this process, hating to lose more than loving to win will place more of your attention on losing than it does on winning. Think about that for a moment. When you set out to attempt to win, it makes you susceptible to thinking more about failure than it does about success. Why would anyone want to do that?

Focusing on losing means that you are far more likely to pay attention to negative thoughts that will encourage your brain to search for negative feelings. That is how the process works and what your brain looks for it usually finds. Therefore, before you compete or attempt something new you begin from the position of paying attention to avoiding a loss rather than focusing on achieving a win. If your inner story is about being the sort of person who hates to lose, feelings associated with losing will also stay around much longer in your mind when you do lose than they would in the mind of the sort of person who loves to win. These feelings place you in danger of having an opponent inside your head. It increases the chances of the 'I' inside your head manipulating the 'Me' inside your head. You may hate to lose, you may have set out feeling full of belief that you will not lose but you are still focusing on losing. Focusing on losing invites your negative and closed inner voice to rise to the occasion.

When this happens you are at risk of being emotionally hijacked by negativity and persistent self-doubt. In any competitive context it is important that you respect your opponent, therefore, you must also respect the potential opponent inside your head too. People who love to win will still feel the pain of losing but will not over-focus on losing. They will move on to learning from what happened and focusing on how they will prepare for the next opportunity to win.

Being the sort of person who hates to lose can make you susceptible in other ways too, for example, in how you are influenced by the negative comments of others.

Imagine that you are asked to give a presentation to eighty people. You feel that you have prepared well and performed well. This has boosted your confidence and made you feel good about your self. As the audience is leaving the room you overhear one person talking to another about your presentation, "that was disjointed and I lost interest. I don't think she put enough thought and preparation into it". If stronger feelings about losing than winning are part of your inner story you could be very sensitive to such a comment. Hearing it can feel devastating. In your mind your thoughts can take you to a place where you imagine other people having the same private conversation about you too. It can even entice your inner voice to convince you that most people who attended your presentation are likely to be having a similar conversation somewhere outside of the room.

Your thoughts and emotions are always on the move and in this situation your thoughts will search out feelings of anxiety to associate with and become attached to. In some situations feeling anxious is a good thing – feeling anxious indicates that you are acknowledging your feelings instead of denying them. There are even times when it is important to be anxious, when you *need* to be anxious, because certain types of anxiety can be stimulating and therefore beneficial for performance. Feeling anxious and engaging with anxiety can ultimately help you to be more relaxed. 'Galvanising anxiety' can be processed by your mind as an indicator that you are ready to perform, it can increase your levels of alertness and speed up your reactions. It can make you feel that you are so completely focused that you cannot wait for the performance to begin. Unfortunately for you, on this occasion your thoughts have become attached to feelings of neurotic anxiety because you are the sort of person who hates to lose. Neurotic anxiety can cause you to become engulfed and entangled by emotions: emotions that you do not want and do not need.

Neurotic anxiety invites fear to flow. Neurotic anxiety can generate angst and as a consequence you will approach your next presentation with a lack of self-confidence. Excessive neurotic anxiety can remain unresolved in your mind unless you accept it and deal with it. It might cause you to avoid putting your self in any future situation where you are required to deliver a presentation. Someone who loves to win will not react in the same way when they encounter negativity.

If you are the sort of person who loves to win then your inner story allows you to perceive the comment differently, especially as you set out to ensure that things went well. In your mind you are focused on your own success and so your thoughts will search for feelings that reinforce your belief and confidence in being a success. This enables you to place the comment in context: one person said it, which means that seventy-nine other people may well have enjoyed the presentation.

If there is an outcome that you want – be it winning a game in a sporting context, winning a pitch in a business context or achieving a particular professional target or a personal goal – being the sort of person who is focused more on winning than they are on losing is an advantage. It is also worth bearing in mind too that people who are focused more on winning than they are on losing tend to be luckier in life. Love to win more than you hate to lose.

Attach the Right Thoughts to the Right Feelings

In your mind thoughts are wandering around on the lookout for like-minded friends to spend time with and become attached to. Those friends that they are searching for, or welcoming with open arms, are your feelings. Thoughts and feelings love to get intimately acquainted with each other inside your mind. They are doing so at this very moment. This is why it is important to tune in to what is going on in your mind and to take control of what thought and feeling associations and partnerships are occurring. Everyone needs to have the right thought and feeling associations to be more successful. Let's take an example of a person who already has a positive view of their ability to win that is backed up by real world evidence about the way that they behave in relation to winning. They might describe this strand of their inner story in the following way,

'I am the sort of person who gives everything to win.'

They also have to know what it means for them to be that sort of person.

In this case,

> "...and this means that I will always remain persistent and
> determined so that I maximise my chance of winning."

One technique for maximising your chance of winning is to be better
at noticing the associations and attachments that are happening in
your mind. When you become more conscious of what is going on
in your mind you are able to take control and ensure that a thought
about being the sort of person who gives everything to win attaches
itself to the right feeling that will increase your chance of winning.

Desire to win

You might choose 'desire' as the feeling you will attach to your
thought. Now 'giving everything to win' is paired up with *'the
desire to win'*. This is a compelling choice of thought and feeling
attachment because the desire to win will drive your levels of
persistence and determination and will increase your chance of
consistently performing at your best. It will also ensure that you
demonstrate the commitment behaviours that are required to
increase your chance of winning. Commitment behaviours are at
the heart of the desire to win.

The mind creates the most beautiful narratives when driven by the
desire to win.

Entitlement to win

Consider what happens when you have the same thought about
giving everything to win but attach a different feeling to it. This
time you chose 'entitlement' – *the entitlement to win*. Now the story
that you tell your self is that you feel entitled to win and therefore
you obviously deserve to win.

With this thought and feeling attachment you instantly increase
the chance that motivation, ambition, performance and results will
be affected negatively. Now the probability of becoming complacent
and of being overconfident or arrogant increases rapidly because
you are being influenced by an ego-driven illusion that you are in
complete control of the outcome. The potential for losing begins

to loom large in this situation because your thoughts and feelings help to create your reality and we perform according to our reality. This specific thought and feeling attachment helps to explain why it is possible for the underdog to beat the champion in competitive sport. Your performance is constructed in your mind. Self-talk, and especially self-speak, contribute to this process, as I will describe in chapter eight. Your mind can be unpredictable at times and to perform at your best you need a consistent alignment between your thoughts and feelings before, during and after any performance. One strand of your inner story that can help you achieve this is – if you want to win show the desire to win in everything that you do.

Focusing on Focus

'Focus' is a word and a concept that I have already used many times. Focus is a popular word in sport, in business and in other areas of life. I hear it often. It is also a concept that is often misunderstood and misused. This raises the question,

'What is focus and what does being focused mean?'

When you are focused you are fully conscious. This is why being focused is often described as "being present" or as "being in the zone". When you are focused you direct your full attention towards whatever you need to pay attention to in the present moment. Being focused means that you are present in the moment, present in your self and can perform at your best no matter what the circumstances are. Being focused is an experience but it is also a skill. You can learn to be better at managing your attention.

When you are focused it is possible to feel so consciously immersed in the present that you experience a mental state where what is happening appears to be taking place in slow motion. In elite sport, when someone's confidence is high and they are performing exceptionally well they sometimes describe how time appears to slow down for them. Time is not only a linear concept that is broken down into segments such as months and days, it is also a personalised experience that takes place inside your mind. How we experience time is influenced by what is going on in our mind, including how we feel. Feeling confident and paying full attention to the present can change a person's perception of time. You may have experienced this particular sensation in sport too. You may have experienced it in life incidents where an unexpected crisis happens; you are the person who feels calm, time feels like it moves slowly and you take control of finding a solution while those around you panic.

To be focused you also need to be aware of potential distractions that will compete for your attention. Some distractions could be internal, such as your thoughts or feelings, others could be external such as the behaviour or performance of your colleagues or teammates. Being able to control distractions will help you to make quicker and better decisions especially when you are under pressure.

When you are focused your brain is hiding what you want it to hide and revealing what you want it to reveal and you are in full control of the patterning process.

Focus on the right thing

Despite what sports commentators and expert analysts in sport might claim, you never "lose focus". You simply focus on the wrong thing. The 'wrong thing' does not necessarily mean a single thought or feeling. It can be a collection of thoughts or feelings about your self, it can be related to thoughts and feelings about others or it can be related to what is happening in your environment. Remember, in your mind all information cannot be equal and your attention likes to shift and drift. Focus can free float if you allow it to and it is always possible for your attention to be misdirected and for you to focus on the wrong thing. Paying attention to how you pay attention is essential if you want to be more successful. You have to know which aspects of reality you need to pay attention to. That is critical to being focused.

There are professions where influencing, misdirecting or exploiting you, so that you focus on the wrong thing, will improve their outcomes. To explore the nature of focus I will choose occupations that depend upon misdirecting your attention: professional magicians and mentalists. To be fair to them many are honest enough to openly tell you that they are going to misdirect you before they go ahead and do it. They know that they are onto a winner if they can direct your attention so that you focus on the wrong thing. Therefore, to improve their art, some will learn about the psychology of influence and persuasion, the role of language in manipulating the mind and become proficient in knowing how to apply perception-without-awareness techniques in order to leave you mystified as to what is happening.

They also know that if they present a choice to someone, there are people who are willing to believe that the choice that they make is a free choice. This renders the person unaware of the more subtle shades of misdirection that have been applied to influence the choice that is made. A choice will certainly feel like it is a free one but there is a strong possibility that it is not. Magicians and mentalists know that if they can influence you to focus on a new reality that they have created in your mind, they can leave you astonished and bewildered as to how a trick happened.

Jokes can help you understand the nature of focus too. Jokes make you laugh because their structure entices you to focus on the wrong thing. You do not lose focus when someone is telling a joke to you; you are being misdirected into focusing on the wrong thing so that you cannot see the punch-line coming. It is also worth mentioning here that making you laugh can also be a technique that is used to misdirect your attention. We rarely perceive people that make us laugh as being either threatening or manipulative. This is why, in medieval times, court jesters were able to say the most provocative and outlandish things to royalty without fear of retribution. Similar principles apply in the trickster and transformer stories that exist within western and eastern folklore and traditions.

If I asked you to draw the 'head' side of a particular coin, making sure the head is facing the correct way, exactly as it is on the coin, you are likely to be poor at completing this task even though you handle coins every day. This is because you do not need to pay full attention to the way that the head is facing on a coin, unless you are a coin enthusiast of course. If the rules were changed tomorrow and you could only spend a coin if you were able to draw which way the head was facing, you would be surprised at how you focus on the right thing and complete the task successfully. That is how focus works. To be focused you have to identify what it is that you need to pay full attention to and why. What you focus on may need to change as your potential for success increases or decreases but you still have to identify what the right thing is.

Focus on the Process More Than the Outcome

In a competitive environment there are four key dimensions to pay attention to when you are preparing to win. They are tactical, technical, physical and psychological. Focusing on the process is a key aspect of the psychological preparation for success.

Have you ever struggled to get to sleep? If you have, then you may well have noticed that the worst thing you can do when you want to get to sleep is to try to get to sleep. When you try in vain to get to sleep it can become frustrating because trying to get to sleep actually keeps you awake. There is a reason for this. Focusing on an outcome that you cannot control does not increase the likelihood of the outcome happening. Focusing even harder on an outcome that you cannot control does not increase the likelihood of the outcome happening either. If you want to sleep then it is better to focus on the *process* that will help you to sleep – becoming more relaxed. When you focus on relaxing you are able to work out how to take control of the process by using techniques such as visual or muscle relaxation. Then you notice that your increasing state of relaxation enables you to start to yawn and begin to drift off to sleep.

When you want to win you inevitably have to think about the outcome – winning – but it will be detrimental to your chances of being successful if you are too focused on winning. If you are over-focused on winning then you are focused on the wrong thing rather than the right thing. The reason for this is that you cannot control whether you win or lose and, psychologically, it is always advantageous to focus on controlling the controllables. If you cannot control it then the best decision is to understand it and let go of it. In a win or lose situation there are many factors beyond your control that will affect whether you win or lose. You will be more successful if you pay attention to controlling what you can control.

Focusing on the process is one of the keys to being more successful. The process can relate to the steps you are taking towards your goal. In a competitive environment it can also mean focusing on enjoying the competition and being competitive. I have worked with some businesses where describing someone as being "process-driven" is often social code for saying that the person is boring. Such companies are missing the point when they frame people who focus on the process in this way. Higher performance and successful results may happen accidentally or coincidentally but they will not happen consistently unless you focus much more on the process than you do on the outcome. If you want to be a winner you have to prepare to win.

I was working with an international footballer who was a player expected to score goals. He was experiencing what is often described as a 'goal drought' and his composure had been affected as a consequence. I soon discovered that he had become over-focused on the outcome – scoring goals – convinced that he was focusing on the right thing. It does seem logical that if you have not scored any goals for some time you should place your full attention on scoring goals. He felt he was in a positive place psychologically because he went into every game believing that today was the day when he would score a goal. He was adopting what he described to me as "a positive mental attitude". Whilst it felt positive to him, focusing on an outcome that you cannot control is actually a problematic mental attitude, especially if the outcome that you want does not happen and does not happen over a period of time. Not surprisingly, having had a run of games where he had not scored any goals, negative thoughts inside his mind were rampantly chasing around looking for emotions to attach to. Inside his mind confidence was becoming fragmented. Forgetting about scoring goals would have been a much better choice and could have kept his confidence intact. If you want to score more goals then forgetting about scoring goals really can be the best decision to make.

For the purpose of brevity I will not go into detail about the deeper psychological processes and constructs that need altering to improve confidence, composure and belief inside someone's mind. Suffice to say that entering the game with a focus on the process – what he was thinking, feeling and doing that enabled him to score goals – worked well for him. Instead of focusing on an outcome that he could not control he began to focus on the process of "threatening the goal" instead. Threatening the goal is a process that is within his control throughout every game and therefore it will help to create and maintain a more relaxed mental state. Thinking about threatening the goal reduced self-generated pressure and increased self-belief. It also changed how he prepared mentally for a game as well as what he focused on during the game. His commitment to changing the way he was thinking and feeling helped to bring the drought to an end. I say 'helped' because psychology contributed to the technical and tactical support he was also receiving at the time – but he was the person who went out onto the pitch and scored the goals. That is where the credit lies.

Motivation and Inspiration

Most people would agree that being more successful and achieving what you want in life requires motivation. To a degree they are right, but motivation, like talent, is not enough. Being the sort of person who is motivated is not sufficient if you want to achieve the success that you desire. To be more successful you need to be consistently motivated.

Being consistently motivated enables you to dig deep to find the resources within you that will help you to achieve what you want to achieve. I say that you have to dig deep within you because motivation begins in your mind and being consistently motivated is fundamentally a lonely activity. It is lonely because you are totally reliant on your mind to consistently create the right thought and feeling associations so that you take action for as long as is required. When you are consistently motivated, at the moment that you decide to take action once again, it is all about you having a dialogue inside your mind. That is when we begin to realise that motivation involves those lonely moments of discussion when it is just you and your mind: an open voice telling you that you can do it and a closed voice that disagrees.

But how do you become consistently motivated?

Motivation and motives

Inside our heads we are all instinctively motivated to think, feel and behave in certain ways in order to protect ourselves and stay secure and alive. Therefore we learn to pull ourselves away from some things and push ourselves towards others.

The word 'motivation' sounds like it relates to our 'motives' in life. If motivation was just about our motives then we would be living in a world where everyone figures out what they want and they just go and get it. Life is not that simple and nor is motivation. Motivation is influenced by your inner story and therefore your thoughts and feelings are always in play both at a conscious and unconscious level. Instead of thinking about motivation being linked to motives, it is far more helpful to think of motivation by combining the three letters at the start of the word and the three letters at end of the word and reflecting on how it is absolutely impossible for 'motivation' to exist without 'motion'. Using the same principle you can also see that 'challenge' cannot exist without 'change'.

<u>Moti</u>vation cannot exist without motion.

<u>Challenge</u> cannot exist without change.

Motivation and motion

Motivation involves being sufficiently energised to challenge your self and change from one state to another. These can be emotional states, physical states or thinking states.

Motivation involves pushing your self towards thinking, feeling or doing something different or differently to help you get to where you want to be. Motivation can involve being pushed by others but consistent motivation will occur when someone is self-determined and able to self-regulate. When you are consistently motivated you do not need others to inspire you to action.

It might be helpful if others provide encouragement but the decision to take action is always going to be the result of the 'Me' and 'I' dialogue that takes place in your mind.

Be inspired and get motivated

I have heard motivation and inspiration talked about as if they are the same. Inspiration and motivation are connected but you can be inspired without ever being motivated. Motivation is not the same as inspiration.

Inspiration involves the stirring of your spirit and the desire and intention to get something done. Motivation involves motion, actually getting something done. The inspiration-motivation relationship is similar to that of imagination and creativity. You can play with a concept or idea, disrupt its orthodoxy and allow your self to imagine what it might be like if it was different. You can also use your imagination to invent something new or you can imagine a new variation on an already known theme. But to make what you imagine become a reality you have to be motivated and take action. You have to be creative; you have to go ahead and create something. There are many imaginative people in the world who feel unfulfilled or full of regrets as a consequence of not being creative. Just like there are many inspired people who feel the same way because they were inspired but they were not motivated.

One popular method of aiming to inspire people to action is to display so-called "motivational" slogans and quotations in environments where motivation matters. These are often a visual dose of try-harder medicine. It is a challenge to find robust and reliable evidence to show that covering environments with such slogans and quotations makes any sustained difference to people's motivation or consistency of motivation. The habituation effect suggests that, in your mind, repetitive processing of quotations and slogans is likely to diminish the usefulness of their impact. Rather than people being regularly inspired and tuning in to the message, they actually become uninspired and tune out instead. It takes much more than a quotation or a slogan to positively alter perception of self or influence mindset and behaviour. This becomes especially problematic when some of these slogans, rather than making the complex simple actually make the complex frivolous. Reading that "winners never quit and quitters never win", for example, might inspire a moment of introspective reflection. On the surface the statement may be inspirational but it is a huge and possibly erroneous assumption to make that it will have a deeper impact on motivation and change behaviour. As an aside, that particular slogan is laced with conceptual confusion too, but that is another matter.

So, the next time that your spirit is stirred, engage with your mind and take action. Be inspired but then make sure that you get motivated. When you decide to take action, take it and commit to being consistently motivated to do so for as long as it takes. Be consistently motivated. Actions improve your chance of success more than intentions ever can and ever will. The outcomes of marketing campaigns for people to join their local gym at the start of a New Year would be less financially lucrative if we were all fully committed to being consistently motivated.

How to be consistently motivated

To be consistently motivated a person must be willing to take full responsibility for their behaviour. They must also accept that motivation involves uncertainty, challenge and unpredictability. Motivation involves being willing to step into the unknown and being willing to embrace uncertainty. It also involves confronting unpredictability because we make mental calculations about our perceived competence and probability of success when we set demanding targets and goals. Within seconds we make projected judgments about our ability to cope and our capacity to rise to the challenge. These calculations will affect self-belief and influence how consistent our levels of mental and physical commitment are. They also affect the nature and quality of the goals that we set. Consistent motivation, like learning, involves emotional risk.

To achieve consistency of motivation it is vital that you stay emotionally balanced during the successes or setbacks that you experience. Progress towards a goal never happens in a straight line; there are always twists and turns and highs and lows on your journey. It is important to celebrate and savour the joy and momentum that the experience of winning creates and to revel in the unadulterated joy of the big wins, but it is also important to learn from the setbacks and losses too. Over-reacting psychologically to winning or losing can reduce your hunger to succeed, dampen your motivation, dilute commitment and misdirect your focus.

There are times when you need to be mentally resilient too.

When I use the word 'resilient' I do not mean resilience as if it is a personality trait, even if it does appear to have trait-like qualities, I mean resilience as a dynamic and fluid process that grows and unfolds in your mind. Resilience is a process that can be nurtured.

Consistent motivation requires us to be resilient. This includes being resilient in those challenging moments when there is no opportunity to come up for air and you just have to be strong enough to battle hard with your self to stay afloat when you feel like you are about to go under. Resilience enables you to be patient and hold your nerve or to be adaptable and find a different way. Again, others may encourage and support you but it is inside your mind where you find the emotional resources to ensure that you finish when the competition finishes and not when you feel that you are unable give any more. Ask your self, "what it is that keeps my mind resilient so that I never let my body have the last word?" Once you know the answer to this question you can call upon those thoughts and emotions to increase your ability to be self-determined and to ensure that you not only enjoy pressure you also thrive under pressure. To win the game you have to be able to stay in the game.

Consistent motivation involves being resilient enough to remain committed for as long as it takes and giving everything that you can in the present to enable you to achieve what you want to achieve in the future. This is particularly important to keep in mind in those situations in sport when preparation routines for competing feel and become mundane and repetitive. It is also important when you know you have to complete a task that you will not enjoy but accept that the task is necessary in relation to achieving your goal. To stay committed there are times when you have to keep the bigger picture in mind, call upon your resilience resources and be willing to adapt your inner story when necessary. Commitment is the key to consistency.

Forget About Your Goal

If you want to be successful you need to have a realistic, achievable and demanding future-focused goal. You need a goal that takes you beyond your comfort zone and one that has real worth and meaning for you so that you are consistently motivated to achieve it. To achieve a goal you have to cross a threshold and you also have to be able to navigate that threshold. Navigating the threshold can be a psychological as well as a physical challenge. I should clarify that when I use the word 'goal' I am describing where you wish to be at the end of any challenge. I should also clarify that when I use the word 'wish' I am not referring to a deluded daydream. I am referring to you realistically and specifically knowing what you wish to achieve and then identifying it in exact terms. If you are setting a goal you should always do so in exact terms. You cannot get to where you want to be just by wishing, otherwise everyone who wishes would end up being world-class at what they do. Wishing, like talent and motivation, is not enough. Being more successful than you currently are involves working as well as wishing.

Achieving a goal is not only about identifying where you start and where you will finish; you also need to have a concept of the work that will be involved along the way. You need an outline of what the journey that you intend to take is going to look like for you. You need a mental map. Your map has to include how you will get from A to B – otherwise you can know your departure and destination points but remain confused about how to navigate your way there. If you want to be more successful than you currently are you will need a map that includes navigation as well as destination. You will never get where you want to be in life if you live in a land with no maps.

No matter what goal fetishists tell you, there is no need to chant your goal at the start of every day or carry around a written version with you wherever you go. You do not have to be a devotee of your goal – you just need to *know* your goal. Knowing your goal will locate it in your mind. When you know what your goal is it does not have to remain in your conscious mind at all times. If your goal rests in your unconscious mind for periods of time that is not only normal it can provide you with a competitive edge and advantage. Consciously over-focusing on your goal can interfere with your ability to achieve it. Neither do you need to obsess about your goal because if you focus too regularly on your goal it can prevent you from identifying the smaller steps that enable you to make progress towards it. There are many psychological and performance benefits in not focusing on your goal. It can help you place your full attention on to navigation so that you are not continually preoccupied with destination. When you know what your goal is, set it and then forget it.

If You Want to Arrive You Have to Travel

In the real world you will not miraculously arrive at your destination heralded by a fanfare of trumpets and a fountain of ticker tape to celebrate your success. Even if you discover that your dreams are closer to you than you initially imagined, you still have to travel to achieve them. Travelling is not always easy. Some of us have to travel much further than others to get to where we want to be. Some of us have to overcome bigger obstacles too. These obstacles can exist in the mind and exist in the external world. The road to success can be bumpy and rough and therefore travelling requires dedication and determination. To reach your goal you must have targets that structure your journey for you and help you to focus on the work that you need to put in along the way. Your targets have to be open to change too so that reaching your destination becomes inevitable. Here the question arises about how you set goals and targets for a journey that could be long and challenging. You do this by starting with two key words. Those two words are "I will". "I am the sort of person who wants to be more successful and this means that *I will...*"

I have had discussions with people who set targets by beginning with "I will try to...". Setting targets with these four words indicates that something at a deeper level is not quite right. In my experience, "I will try to..." is usually an unconscious expression of a person's lack of self-belief in their capacity to succeed. At times it can also illuminate a lack of faith in their personal levels of commitment. The phrase "I will try to..." also allows a person to look elsewhere for reasons and explanations as to why she or he did not achieve what they wanted to achieve. This immediately increases the potential for them to search for external rather than internal accountability. As a result they can create excuses, blame their environment and accuse other people for their own lack of personal success. If only their coach, their boss or their team leader had done something differently, then success would have happened.

Instead of looking in the mirror and honestly asking, "what

could I have done differently and better?" their first focus is away from the mirror. If you have an excuse lined up before you attempt a challenge you are far more likely to use it when times get tough.

When you set out to be more successful always express a goal or a target with "I will...". The word 'I' demonstrates that you are taking responsibility, control and ownership of achieving your goal. This means that you will consider your own accountability if you struggle to reach your goal or do not reach it. It also means that you will increase your confidence and self-belief when you do achieve your goal. The word 'will' is a powerful word in anyone's inner story because in your mind it creates a forward projection of success. There are times when others set the parameters of success for you by telling you how far you have to travel in order to succeed. They inform you that if you reach a certain point on your journey it will mean that you are successful in their eyes and on their terms. They define success for you and set the limits on how far you have to travel before you arrive. If you find your self in this situation then remember that success on your terms is what matters. They may have set the target too low for you and the destination too close to you. If that is the case it is important to travel further, aim higher and arrive at a better place. Exceed expectations.

There are many different ways of travelling. You have to figure out what works best for you in your world and if it works well do more of it. What follows is an example of how someone used what worked for him to ensure that he became more successful.

Less than the blink of an eye
John Naber was a member of the USA Olympic swim team. He was part of the winning 100m Backstroke semi-final relay team in Munich but was not selected to represent his country in the final.

John dealt with this setback by being determined to return at the following Olympics in four years time in Montreal and win a gold medal in the relay event. John was ambitious, he also set his sights on winning a gold in the individual event too. From looking at a breadth of performance and progress data John calculated that he would need to complete the 100m Backstroke in 55.5 seconds to win a gold medal in the individual event in four years time. The challenge for John was that his current personal best performance in the 100m Backstroke was 59.5 seconds.

To be the best in the world at 100m Backstroke in four years time he had to improve his personal best by four seconds. That was how far John had to travel before he could arrive. A four second improvement in a 100m race seems like an impossible task – unless John focused on the right thing for him. John believed that he could make this journey a successful one if he broke down his goal into smaller targets. This is how he did it. If he had to improve by four seconds over four years that meant he had to improve his performance by one second *every year*. This feels like a daunting task, so John continued to break down the target. At that time John was training for ten months each year. This meant that he would have to achieve a one-tenth of a second improvement in his performance *every month*. As there were approximately thirty days in each of the months in which he trained he calculated that he would have to improve his performance by 1/300th of a second *every day*.

Now achieving his dream of a gold medal seemed far more possible. John trained four times a day so this meant that he could aim for 1/1200th of a second improvement in *every session*. Instead of focusing on what he needed to do in four years time, John established that, in each training session, he had to make an improvement in his performance that was less than the blink of an eye.

For the next four years John travelled so that he could arrive. He achieved his goal of winning a gold medal as part of the relay team in Montreal in 1976. He also reached the final of the individual event and competed against the current Olympic champion. Not only did John win a gold medal in that event too, he also created a new world record. His time... 55.49 seconds.

Honesty Really is the Best Policy

Research has shown that we are very good at remembering what we see at the end of a list or at the end of a sequence. This is why I have deliberately included one of the most important strands of an inner story for success at the end of this chapter.

I know from my professional experience that those people who consistently perform at an elite level are always willing to evaluate their own performance and progress honestly. They take an honest look at every performance. Doing this involves making an assessment that is as objective as possible so that they are open to accepting what real world evidence is telling them about how they are performing and progressing towards a target or goal.

Being the sort of person who takes an honest look at your own performance and progress means that you will focus on the right thing, control and execute the right process and navigate towards a successful destination.

The Short Story

Success involves working as well as wishing.

If you want to arrive you have to travel.

You do not lose focus – you focus on the wrong thing.

Forgetting your goal can help you to achieve it.

Being willing to fail increases your chance of success.

Pay attention to the process more than the outcome.

Love to win more than you hate to lose.

Assess your performance as honestly and as objectively as possible.

You will never get to where you want to be if you live in a land with no maps.

Motivation is not enough. Consistent motivation is.

Chapter Seven
Being Happier

When offered the opportunity to change their inner story people often want to have a better personal relationship with happiness. They want to feel happier or be happier or they want an answer to the question "how do I become happier?" Happiness is an emotion that we strive for.

In this chapter I will, amongst other things, show you how forgetting about happiness can make you happier, explain why Premiership footballers can get depressed, ask whether you look at happiness in a vertical or a horizontal way, stress the importance of kindness and suggest that most people who are angry need non-anger management. But first of all, let's explore how we can become happier and get to the essence of what happiness is so that you can be the sort of person who knows what will make you happier and are able to decide how you can become happier.

As your mind is so important in relation to your happiness it is helpful to understand it better, especially in relation to knowing how what is going on in there creates your moods and your emotions. It is also important for you to know how your mind influences your perception of your world.

Your perception of what is happening to you affects your emotions far more than what is actually happening to you.

How your mind interprets what is happening in your world has a bigger impact on your feelings than what is *really* happening in your world.

Perception is Not Reality

Happiness depends on perception. Allow me to explain why perception is so important by highlighting the relationship between loneliness and happiness. Loneliness is more of a psychological state than a physical state. If I see that you are on your own that does not mean I should perceive that you are lonely and therefore unhappy. In my mind I might think that being alone makes a person feel lonely and therefore makes them potentially unhappy. From my perspective this seems like a reasonable thought to have, after all, most people smile and laugh much more when they are with others than they do on their own. However, in your mind you might feel that being on your own offers you a time of welcome peace and solitude and feel very happy about that.

I might see you with some friends that you know well and assume that people in such situations are happy. After all, we are social beings and one person's happiness within a group can spread and make others feel happy too. As a consequence, I perceive that you must be happy and if someone else in the group looks to me as if they are in a happy mood I might assume that this could make you feel even happier. Yet, even though you are part of a social group, inside your mind you may be feeling isolated and lonely. Again, what I perceive to be happening is not necessarily what is really happening. This is because your brain is busy constructing your perceptions and my brain is busy constructing mine. What we perceive we tend to believe but that is not the full story because perception is complex.

The popular mantra states that 'perception is reality' but perception is not reality, as I have just tried to demonstrate. Perception is the lens or the filter that creates your connection to your reality and my connection to my reality. We perceive and interpret the world from the standpoint of our inner story. This is why it is always possible for you to misinterpret what you are sensing and seeing. Although it is tempting, we cannot make assumptions about how someone is feeling based solely upon our perceptions of how we think we would feel if we were in their context or situation and then believe those assumptions to be true.

Why now?

Another popular mantra states that what you see is what you get. However, what you see is not what you get. What we perceive cannot be taken for granted. This is highly relevant when you begin to consider how to become happy or happier because you have to analyse your perception of what it is that is making you feel unhappy. When you do this you really need to focus on the present. What is it that is making me unhappy now? Events in the past may have an impact on how you feel today. It is always possible that your past can make you feel unhappy in the present but you can change your inner story by viewing or framing the past in a different way. This can help you to feel happier now, today. You can become the sort of person who is not willing to give what happened in your past, or regrets about your past, the permission to dictate your feelings in the present.

When I talk with people who tell me that they want to be happier I recommend that they focus on the present because they can be predisposed to believe that because they may have been unhappy for some time, they will continue to remain unhappy in the future. Imagining and projecting unhappiness into the future is without doubt a self-defeating activity because the future by nature is uncertain, the future is unpredictable and, get ready for a staggeringly obvious but highly pertinent point, the future has not happened yet. Let's be honest, if you are searching for a solution within the unpredictability of something that you can only imagine because it does not exist yet, it is unlikely to be the most fruitful and reliable route to feeling better. Focusing on the future can cause you to become absent from the present. Focusing on the present enables you to be more present and ask the critical question "why now?". This vital question allows you to explore what it is that has caused you to want to do something about being happier today.

I also suggest to people that the fastest way to become happier is to forget about happiness. Unless they know me they often look puzzled and think that I have lost the plot. You may have that reaction too. My reason, which is based upon how the mind works, is this – if you desire or need something, you have to know what that something is and you have to know what that something means to you. In the context we are exploring here, you have to work out what happiness is and what happiness means to you.

Just as you have to explore why we behave the way we do to understand why you behave the way you do, you have to explore how we can become happier so that you can become happier. You may do this by comparing your happiness to that of people that you know and consider what makes them happy or unhappy. You could also relate to stories you have heard or read about what it is that makes other people happy. You gather all of this information and change it from information into knowledge by applying it to your life. Inside your mind information can become knowledge and, as you apply knowledge over time, knowledge can become wisdom. You already know that I am going to ask you to forget about happiness but before I do that let's consider what happiness is.

What is Happiness?

You can feel, experience and express happiness and you can also see and hear it in others, but what is it? What is happiness? Defining happiness and how to achieve it has challenged the minds of philosophers, psychologists and spiritual leaders for centuries. For now, let's stick with the philosophers and consider what some philosophers have proposed. What do they think happiness is? Can philosophy help us to discover what happiness is and how we might attain it? Here are some of their perspectives.

It can be proposed that achieving happiness is the ultimate aim of being alive. However, it can also be proposed that the mere action of thinking about how to become happier proves that as humans we are not meant to be happy at all. If you have to think about being happier then happiness is clearly not a natural state of being for humans. Here the philosophical argument is that we should abandon our aspirational expectations for increased levels of happiness and focus on reducing our fears and anxieties instead. By doing this we come to acknowledge and accept how angst-ridden life really is. Instead of trying to be happier, and constantly seeking pleasure by avoiding pain, we should pay more attention to preparing ourselves for dealing with the disappointments that life will inevitably bring. This enables us to gain deeper levels of insight into the nature of the human condition, allows us to manage adversity and ultimately furnishes us with wisdom.

That philosophical position may not have cheered you up and I certainly have no intention of bringing your mood down further, but, some philosophers have proposed that each day we should spend a small amount of time reflecting on thoughts about the loss of those we love and value. The position taken here is that thinking about the moment that we will lose our loved ones reminds us to deeply appreciate, savour and enjoy their love and friendship now. Thinking about loss and grief increases your insight into how life is precious and how it could be much worse than it feels right now. It may seem paradoxical but the view here is that thinking about grief can make you happier and also focuses your mind on what you have that you can be grateful for. Aspects of gratitude can also be dependent upon how your inner story interacts with the inner story of others and therefore you can increase your happiness further not only by being grateful but also by expressing your gratitude to your self and to others. Remember, expressing gratitude is one way of affirming what is positive in your life and as a consequence it can increase happiness, enrich relationships and boost your sense of connectedness.

It has also been proposed that happiness itself is not enough to make you happy. You need to make the right choices in order to be happier. For example, choosing to live a virtuous life – which includes being compassionate to others – rather than a life defined by the pursuit of pleasure. This will offer more potential for creating lasting happiness. Philosophers also propose that we can only become happier through a long-term quest: a pursuit for happiness. Some insist that this pursuit must involve pain, suffering and personal hardship. Experiencing emotional pain, suffering, misery and a lack of connectedness is seen as essential here as it enables us to gain a deeper meaning in our lives and to be far more appreciative of happiness when we ultimately discover it. You can not really appreciate winning until you have lost.

It has been proposed that if we embark upon a quest for happiness we are searching in the wrong place. Focusing on attaining happiness is focusing on the wrong thing. Perhaps life would be better if we were to focus on achieving other emotional states such as tranquility, inner-peace or even detachment? Then again, being less detached and able to develop greater self-knowledge has been suggested as the key to happiness too.

There are groups proposing that 'happiness' should be an integral component of the social and emotional curriculum in schools. The proposition here is that we can be taught how to be happy and therefore we can learn how to be happy. Learning to be happy is an interesting notion but education does not end when people leave school. If we can learn to be happy then maybe doing so should be a key component of lifelong learning too.

The mindfulness movement has promoted the importance of the Buddhist concept of focusing on the experience of now as it is presented to you, being aware of the moment, being 'mindful'. Mindfulness has become a popular approach for interventions that relate to aspects of psychological health and wellbeing. It is also becoming of increasing interest to psychological research communities. The proposition is that you have to become more mindful to gain clarity, insight and openness into what is happening and accumulating in your mind. To be mindful you have to focus on the right thing in the right way. The practice of meditation is central to this process but mindfulness is not solely located within moments of meditation.

Meditation and mindfulness are interacting components of the noble eightfold path in Buddhism. Whereas the concept of wu-wei in Buddhism is about non-purposive action the concept of mindfulness in Buddhism is about purposive attention. Both concepts involve relaxing into the moment. Misinterpreting what mindfulness is remains possible when an ancient Eastern spiritual practice transforms into a modern Western secular practice. Whilst it can be claimed that mindfulness can lead to happiness through a nurturing of self-compassion it can also be claimed that happiness might not be relevant in achieving a state of enlightened awareness.

The positive psychology movement has also challenged existing notions of happiness too. Positive psychology does not accept that happiness is about the alleviation, removal or absence of misery and suggests that it is more about being able to flourish and be more engaged and fulfilled. It has proposed that improved wellbeing is not only a plausible personal goal it is also an achievable goal for organisations and societies. Positive psychology is seen as being based upon 'the science of happiness'. We can also look wider than the science of happiness because functional and structural neuroimaging, where technology enables us to view and analyse complex brain activity, now allows us to explore the neuroscience of happiness too.

As teachers who work with children who present with challenging behaviour know, it is not the occasional big behavioural incident that is stressful and wears you down, it is the persistent smaller low-level disruptive incidents that do that to you. This raises a question about the possibility that it might not be the occasional big happiness incidents that make you happier – perhaps it is the smaller and more regular incidents that will do that?

As you can see, there are many positions and perspectives on happiness.

The happy life

As a psychologist I am regularly invited inside the minds of people who are confronting or dealing with specific types of personal challenges that can be brought on by significant life challenges. Most have an idea of their preferred outcome: a goal that they wish to achieve. For some this goal relates to feeling differently, to being in a different emotional state than their current state. They often say something like,

> "I am unhappy and I want to be happy."
> "I'd like to become a happier person."
> "If only I felt happier I would be able to..."

Some emotionally agitated people I meet want to move rapidly from being unhappy to being happy. They want to *be* happier. Inside their minds happiness is seen as a remedy for all misfortunes, struggles and anxieties. They imagine a quick fix and fast-track solution that will take them from unhappiness straight to happiness at breakneck speed. They are both impatient and restless in their desire to attain what appears to me to be an all-pervading every-hour-of-the-day state of happiness. You could say that they want to live the happy life.

The difficulty with their forlorn longing for a permanently happy life is that this imagined mental state can only exist if they refuse to accept the existence of impermanence, complexity, injustice, pain and suffering in life. Denying these factors also abandons the need for us to find the courage and resilience deep within us that will help us to deal with adverse life events when we encounter them.

Impermanence is relevant in relation to being or becoming happier. Happy times as well as difficult times are going to be impermanent. That is important to be mindful of when you experience difficult times in your life as it can assist you in developing the resilience and resolve to stay strong, or to stay afloat, so that you can come out the other side of the experience stronger and more able to cope in the future. Being aware of impermanence is also relevant when times are good as it allows you to savour happy times when you experience them, to seize the moment and to have a deeper enjoyment of happy times. Striving for a form of full-on around-the-clock happiness is like striving for perfection: it is not only mentally exhausting it is also unattainable.

A happier life

I also meet people who are less agitated and more realistic. They already know in which areas of life they would like a shift in happiness. Rather than being happier they want to *become* happier. Instead of chasing the happy life they are looking for a happier life. They are more accepting of human vulnerabilities and have more realistic emotional aspirations regarding what matters to them in their life and how that relates to their emotional wellbeing. There are other people that I meet who are looking for happier days in their life. They want to *feel* happier. This can be expressed as wanting to become more upbeat, more satisfied or to be more present in their daily lives so that they can change from a limiting emotional state to a more enabling one. This is usually because a small emotional change will allow them to get something done.

As you can see, my mind has arranged the desired states for increased happiness that I encounter as a psychologist into three categories,

> The happy life
> A happier life
> Happier days

These all exist within a person's own mental timeframe. However, the key factor that I want to highlight is not the timeframe. In all of these situations what is vital is how a person defines happiness because happiness is a subjective concept that is constructed in your mind.

For example, do material possessions make you feel happier than emotional experiences do? Do you think that more individual freedom and less individual responsibility would make you happier? Do you think that thinking about the possibility of becoming a parent will make you happier? Do you think that being a parent will make you happier? The answers to these questions reside in your mind. They might help prompt you to be able to answer the following key questions regarding happiness: what does happiness mean to you? what would make you happier?

You can answer these questions here:

Horizontal and Vertical Happiness

'Happiness' is just like 'self-esteem', it is a big concept that is about all of you. That is why if you want to be happy you have to define what happiness is to you and then break the concept down. One way is to consider happiness as being horizontal and vertical.

You might define happiness in terms of its horizontal nature. By horizontal I mean taking a perspective on the breadth of categories that you attach to happiness: for example social, spiritual, sexual, economic, emotional or medical happiness. You might continue to look laterally but this time look across the breadth of people that you know and benchmark your personal happiness by considering how happy you are in comparison to how happy you think your friends are. You may apply the horizontal perspective to how happy you feel when you retrospectively look across the breadth of your life. You may have reinterpreted particular experiences in your life and see greater value in what felt like insignificant events at the time but turned out to be the big events on your timeline now that you look back on them. Here you take the long view when defining happiness. Has my life been happy so far?

You might define happiness in terms of its vertical nature. By vertical I mean the depth of happiness that you desire or do not desire in your life. You may want less or more of an emotion in your life so that you can feel or be happier: for example less troubled and pessimistic or more satisfied and grateful. You can also define happiness vertically in terms of your life, almost like an arrow pointing down to where you are now on your timeline:

How happy am I today?
How happy was I yesterday?
How happy will I be tomorrow?

Here you take the short view when defining happiness. Happiness is a subjective phenomenon and a subjective wellbeing phenomenon, therefore only you can know what the meaning of happiness is to you. You may want aspects of vertical happiness, you may want aspects of horizontal happiness and, of course, you may want to focus on a combination of both.

How Do We Become Happy?

Psychologists have created a happiness formula that offers one way of understanding what determines our happiness and therefore identifies how we can become happier. The formula provides a framework for reflecting on happiness. It has three key elements, which I describe as follows,

Happiness is determined by how your mind creates your general outlook or orientation on life. For example, you might be in a difficult situation in your life but your outlook on life could still be positive.

Happiness is determined by the opportunities that you have to make voluntary choices that give you more control over your life. As your sense of autonomy, purpose and meaning increases, so do your levels of happiness.

Happiness is determined by factors that are fixed (such as your age) and factors that are fluid (such as your health and your wealth).

Why Premiership footballers can get depressed

If happiness is determined by how your brain and your mind create your outlook on life, this means that happiness is constantly being constructed inside your head. The question here is how much of your happiness is based upon what is going on inside your head? The answer is that most of your happiness is constructed inside your head. Stop for a moment and think about that. As I stated at the outset of this chapter, your happiness depends upon how you perceive your world. Now we are focusing in on happiness and we are adding an extra word to that statement – *most* of your happiness depends upon how you perceive your world.

Most of your happiness depends upon what you decide to focus on and pay full attention to in your life. Only a small amount of your happiness depends upon factors that are outside of your head such as where you live, the type of house you live in and your material possessions. Some psychologists would argue that as little as ten percent of your happiness depends upon factors that exist outside of your head. This helps us understand why Premiership footballers can get depressed and impoverished children can get happier. A Premiership footballer may have gained all of the material possessions that he imagined and needs. Material possessions might offer psychological comfort or reflected status but they do not ensure happiness. He may receive adulation bordering on worship from the public but that might not ensure happiness either. What really matters is what is going on inside his head. If his outlook on life becomes negative, his sense of individual purpose and meaning becomes fragile and his sense of self begins to fragment, he can become depressed. The same applies to any person who has a similar form of celebrity status. Therefore, if we now return to the philosophical idea that happiness is something that we must search for in life, and assume that happiness can be pursued, you are likely to achieve a much better outcome if you search for it inside rather than outside your head.

Look at happiness differently

If people tell me that they are unhappy and would like to be happier, then I ask them to look at happiness differently. Looking differently is an important life skill that can help you to change your world. It allows you to discover new understandings and find new solutions. Sometimes, when we are unhappy we look back to what previously made us happy and attempt to recreate past happiness. This may well turn out to be a flawed strategy because it does not take into account that your self is always changing. When we start to look differently, we consider new ways of being happy *now*, in the present. This also allows us to think about what we could do now – that we have not done before – that will help us to be happier. It challenges us to look at our orientation and perspective on happiness and to change it now. This is one way of looking at happiness differently.

In my professional role I regularly ask people to look differently. What do I mean by 'looking differently'? Here is an example: when you look differently you become aware that, although it may seem paradoxical, both marriage and divorce can contribute to human happiness. Here is another example of what I mean: I sometimes meet people who tell me that they need anger management. When I encourage them to look differently they come to realise that they do not need anger management at all, what they really are in need of is non-anger management. They need to look at how their feelings accumulate inside their mind and how anger moves within their mind. They need to do this because this is the process that causes them to present with angry behaviour.

In this situation some people need non-anger management to help them understand the triggers provoking their anger and why those specific triggers are so powerful. They need to understand the accumulation of feelings that create their anger so that they can begin to change how they feel in a step-by-step manner. This prevents them getting to the point at which they feel overwhelmed and they lose control.

If you want to be happier forget about happiness
The world would be devoid of diversity, bereft of creativity and mind-numbingly tedious if we all looked at everything in the same way from the same place and from the same direction. There are always many ways of looking available to you. My recommendation to people who ask me about becoming happier, and my recommendation to you, is that if you want to be happier

then look at happiness differently. Instead of looking at happiness as involving the elimination of unwanted feelings like sadness or anxiety or being better at chasing and finding pleasure, think of it differently. I suggest that you look at it so differently that you completely forget about happiness because forgetting about happiness can make you feel so much better. I have mentioned in chapter six that if you have difficulties sleeping the best thing you can do is to forget about trying to sleep. Actively forgetting can be very powerful. Similarly, there are other times when it is important to remember to forget. You already know that if you forget about the outcome you can focus more on the process and one process that helps you to be happier relates to changing the feelings that gather together inside your mind and prevent you from being happy: your mood. If you want to be happier forget about happiness and focus on your mood instead.

Focusing on happiness reminds you how miserable you feel
Your brain will often make meaning of what something is by first of all establishing what that something is not. To help you to understand and experience what I mean ask your self this question 'what is the opposite of happy?' and see what answer you come up with.

You may not have thought of a word like 'inhibited' or 'serious'. It is far more likely that you think the opposite of happy is 'unhappy' or 'sad'. Can you see what is happening here? Focusing on happiness actually brings unhappiness and sadness more into your conscious awareness. When you are trying to be happier you run the risk of reminding your self exactly how miserable you feel. Thinking about happiness can induce misery in exactly the same way that using anti-wrinkle cream invites you to notice how wrinkled you are and purchasing age-defying products reminds you that you are getting older by the day. If you want to feel happier, forget about happiness – changing the focus of your attention can help you to become happier. If you want to feel happier, forget about happiness – it's just too big. Break it down and focus on the process that will make you feel better. One way of feeling better is to focus on your mood and how you can change it.

If you focus on changing your mood then you are instantly freed from the daunting, discouraging and totally unrealistic task of taking a gigantic leap from 'unhappy' to 'happy'.

Understand Your Mood

To be able to change your mood, to give your self even the smallest psychological lift, you have to be able to have a better understanding of your mood. A mood is created when accumulated positive or negative emotions decide that they want to hang around together in your mind. When emotions spend time together they create moods. You may not even be aware that emotions are connecting with each other, that they are hiding under each other and gathering together in your mind to create a mood. All of these mood connections and communications are complex and occur in your mind without your conscious awareness.

Your mood spends time building up in your unconscious mind. Not only can a lingering mood in your unconscious mind affect how often you shop and where you shop, it can also influence what you choose to buy and how what you buy impacts upon your sense of identity when you wear it. It can persuade you to engage with some people and not with others. It can cause you to infer all sorts of intentions from the behaviour of others including intentions they never intended. Depending on your mood a 'good morning' nod from a boss, instead of the usually cheerful "Hey, how are you?" that you are used to, can be inferred as dismissive and an indication that you have done something to upset them or that you have suddenly and mysteriously, for no reason that you can think of, become less significant in their world.

In a different mood you might process the nod as being about them rushing around or being preoccupied with what is happening in their world. Moods can be contagious. One person's mood can influence and alter the mood of others. Your mood can even have a detrimental impact on your immune system. All of this can happen without you being consciously aware that a mood is present in your mind. As we will be considering how to change your mood my focus will be on moods that can become debilitating.

When you experience such a mood you may begin to notice a simmering sadness or a rumbling resentment. You may notice that you are more impulsive or irritated than usual or you may just have a general and vague sense of feeling low. It is of value to know how moods develop because, although moods are temporary, they are capable of remaining in your mind longer than emotions can. Being aware of moods can help you to deal with them and prevent the intensity of the reaction that you feel at the point when the mood breaks.

An unwanted surprise

I recall setting off for work one morning, a few months after my mum had died. I was the psychologist for a sports team at the time. I believe that, whenever it is possible to do so, you should keep personal challenges separate from your professional life so that you can give full attention and commitment to your job while you are doing it. Whilst some psychologists are undoubtedly wounded healers, you do not want to see them breaking down into an incoherent heap in front of you when they are supposed to be meeting *your* emotional needs.

I jumped into my car and automatically turned on the radio although I was not consciously aware of doing so. I started to drive to work – fortunately I was consciously aware of doing that. Music drifted into my conscious mind and I began to listen to what I could hear. I recognised the song and started to pay attention to the lyrics. Suddenly I felt emotionally overwhelmed and emotionally empty at exactly the same time. My attention was drawn to a tear that was gathering momentum as it tumbled from my eye and began to slide down my cheek. That tear was the snowflake that caused the avalanche. I stopped the car. Soon I was involved in the type of crying that sends messages back-and-forth to your brain telling it to invite the whole of your upper body to join in. All of this took less than a few minutes to happen.

The surprise for me that day was my sudden discovery of the intensity of a mood that had decided to fill those spaces in your mind that become profoundly silent and echo with emptiness when you experience grief. On reflection, I can see that my mood was present in my mind not only because my mum had died but also because I had not changed my inner story enough after she died. I still needed to be able to understand happiness and grief differently. I also needed to identify and accept exactly what I had lost, that I could never get back, now that my mum was no longer there. Inside my mind a combination of grief-related emotions had clearly been communicating and gathering together for some time. Confusion and emptiness took the opportunity to lead the pack.

Like-minded feelings

A mood is like a wave, it builds before it breaks. So, let's imagine that you feel irritated about a particular aspect of what is happening in your life, such as thinking that people at work no longer take your ideas and views seriously. You already know that in such a situation your brain will help you to search for and find examples of where people appear not to be listening to you. It may also pattern inaccurately so that some people who are actually listening to your ideas may seem to be undermining or ignoring them; all it takes is a lack of eye contact or your misinterpretation of their body language.

Imagine that you feel irritable and your irritability is making you unhappy. Over time, the feeling of irritation becomes more intense and more emotions join in. Irritation becomes frustration. When other emotions become involved in the get-together frustration becomes anger. Remember, anger is not a pure emotion; it contains many feelings that have connected with each other and blended into anger over time. You are now in an angry mood and instead of thinking that your ideas and views are not being taken seriously the feelings that are gathering together and gaining momentum in your mind start to seduce you into personalising what is happening. Now you think that people are not taking *you* seriously. This will increase the intensity of your mood.

As your mood will influence your behaviour, you may start to communicate your anger through your behaviour. When I worked with young children I would explain anger to them by asking them to imagine that they were able to walk around inside their mind. I explained that they would see lots of feelings wandering about on their own looking for like-minded feelings. 'Disappointment' might meet 'upset' and then they both bump into 'hostile'. They continue to meet other associated feelings until they are all gathered together like a gang on a street corner. Like all gangs, some are leaders and some hide between each other amongst the pack – until they all decide to react together as a group. That is anger: lots of different feelings all joining together in your mind to make you feel angry and telling you to behave in a particular way. This developed their emotional knowledge and literacy and helped them to understand that if you want to deal with your anger you can begin by looking at the feelings that create anger for you. The same process applies to happiness.

I would also explain to them that anger may be hanging around in your head for some time and when this happens it puts you into an angry mood. You may not be able to identify the emotions that are causing your mood. You may have no idea why you are in such a mood and you may not even be conscious of the mood, but that does not stop it hanging around for days. That is why you might suddenly become enraged about something that rationally appears to be quite small or trivial – because really you are angry about something else that has been rumbling and tumbling in your mind for some time. It is often difficult to control the breaking point at which you become angry, as it is not always a conscious decision.

What if you want to lift your self out of the anger and start to feel happier? How do you start to feel differently? What can you do to change the mood that you are in? If you define the opposite of angry as calm, then getting from angry to calm in one easy step is as difficult to achieve as getting from unhappy to happy. I would like to suggest that there is a different solution.

Down, Low or Flat? Then Lift Your mood

When you want to make a change you always have to start somewhere. You have to make a choice. The choice I am recommending is a choice that every person can make – a choice to feel differently. People often describe unhappiness as 'feeling low' or 'feeling down' or 'feeling flat'. This is a useful starting point for change because instead of being preoccupied with the unattainable task of getting from unhappy to happy, you focus on your feelings and lift your mood instead. This will help you to feel less low, less down or less flat. Lifting your mood allows you to think about how to become happy rather than suddenly be happy.

If you tell me that you are no longer feeling unhappy it does not necessarily mean that I should assume that you are now feeling happy. The gap between unhappy and happy is wide and crossing it in one leap is an unattainable feat. Lifting your mood offers the opportunity to take smaller steps, alter aspects of your current emotional state and notice how your mood is changing. To lift your mood you look inwards and examine what is going on in your mind and learn to be present in, and accepting of, your feelings. Then you can lift your mood in a step-by-step way. In this case you would identify and examine the feelings that are creating your anger and then understand and, if possible, eliminate them one by one. You can take control of lifting your mood and doing so will increase your happiness. For some people this step-by-step method can be quite a challenging task to conduct on their own and they may require help in doing so. What should they do?

There is always a different way of looking available to you, and it might be best to target your anger in a different way. You can look at all of the areas of your life where you feel angry and choose a priority area where it is most beneficial to make a change and lift that area first. Your priority area may be, "I would like to be calmer around my family". Your family is a priority to you. You do not want to be angry around them and being calmer around them is the area that you immerse your self in. When you notice that your mood is changing, you amplify the change by doing more of what you are doing that is working well for you. You will notice how you begin to feel happier too. "I'd like to be calmer at work" might be your next priority. Once calmer you can try focusing on engaging in non-anger management. This allows you to intervene early when you are conscious that feelings are accumulating in your mind. You can address those feelings so that you can prevent them from leading to anger.

What does lifting your mood look like?

You need to know what lifting your mood looks like for you. You also need to know what part of your mood you think needs lifting. Finally, you need to know how much lifting is the right amount for you to feel better and happier. One way of knowing how to go about lifting your mood is to imagine what you are doing, feeling and thinking when your mood is lifted. Ask your self, if someone were filming me when my mood is lifted what would be happening in that film? What would I be thinking and how would they know what I was thinking? What would I be feeling and what would I be doing differently than I am now? Write your answers down. You might prefer to draw what will be happening when your mood is lifted. Both actions are more permanent than just thinking or talking about it.

You can do that here:

Where to start

The natural place to start when lifting your mood seems to be to change how you think. That is a good place to start but it might not be the best starting place for you. A thought can change a feeling, but a feeling can also change a thought. If changing how you feel is easier for you then do that instead. Feelings have a big impact on creating your conscious mind so changing how you feel will help you to change how you think. Changing your feelings also helps to combat the progressive emotional numbness that people can experience when their mood needs lifting.

You may be the sort of person who believes that motion changes emotion and lifts your mood by changing what you do. If you want to start there then that's fine too – go and do something different or differently. What matters most at this point is that you go beyond an emotional state of intending or committing to take action to a physical state of taking action. There should be a short gap between deciding to take action and taking it because you always have to take some kind of action in order to make a change. If you do not take action then you will remain in, or on the edges of, the emotional state that you do not want to be in. That will not increase your happiness.

142

You also have to decide how much lifting of your mood is required for you? Is it one percent, five percent, ten percent or more? What is good enough for you to help you to start to make a change? Only you can know.

The Value of Kindness

Another way to lift your mood is to be kind to your self. Being kind to your self will help you to become happier. The action that you take to lift your mood does not always have to be about what you do for your self. Kind actions towards others can also lift your mood and have a wider uplifting effect upon your subjective sense of emotional wellbeing too. Random acts of kindness can increase levels of happiness for the people who are involved in the act of being kind as well as the recipients of the kindness.

Even remembering when you have been kind to others will lift your mood. Remembering kind acts you have carried out also increases your desire to continue being kind to others. Being kind will have the effect of strengthening your sense of identity too. Thinking about how you have increased the happiness of others strengthens your private self and kind actions towards others can strengthen your concept of public self. Being kind offers many wellbeing benefits.

I am aware that what I have said could be interpreted as if I am encouraging you to be kind for selfish reasons and therefore it could look also like I am disregarding altruistic acts of kindness: those acts of kindness that are often defined as 'selfless'. There is a conceptual problem in this definition. Acts of kindness cannot be selfless, or as I would say 'self less', as your self is always active to varying degrees when you make a decision to be kind. Kindness begins in your mind and therefore your self will always be involved and invested in acts of kindness. Self will always be connected to kind acts but self-interest does not have to be.

In my view, what is important is the intentionality of your kindness. A kind act can be deliberately intended as 'other-focused' rather than 'self-focused'. It can also be about more than lifting someone else's mood – some people need lifting up while others will need pulling through. When you are engulfed by life's challenges being able to get through on your own can feel and seem overwhelming and an act of kindness, or even kind and respectful words, can travel a long way. In these situations the deliberate intention of your kindness does not have to be attached to self-interest at all and nor does the intentionality have to be dependent upon gratitude, plaudits or the reciprocal response that your kindness receives.

While we are reflecting on kindness, let's consider the perennial question of whether money can buy you happiness. It seems fair to assume that having more money than you currently have will make you happier. In most circumstances it might alleviate stress, provide you with increased choices and freedom and therefore increase your life satisfaction. It also seems fair to assume that having less money than you currently have will not increase your happiness in most circumstances. The generous act of giving money to others who are in need is going to increase your happiness and so will buying a gift for somebody else. However, if most of your happiness is constructed in your mind then money cannot buy you most of your happiness.

It is not only about material generosity either; you can be emotionally generous, energy generous, thought generous and time generous as well. You can cultivate multiple ways of being kind. The nature of your kindness is relevant too. Kindness that is offered from a place of active conscious choice, rather than from a sense of moral duty, is the deepest form of kindness. Kindness can change your world, it can change someone else's world and it can also change the world. Being kind is at the core of what it means to be human. Whenever it is possible, kindness should always have the last word.

Focus on Your Feelings

Striving to attain happiness and avoid unhappiness is like being on a diet. People can lose weight only to find that at a later point their weight increases again and a cyclical loss-gain pattern is established. This is because people who diet are often focused on the wrong thing. They really would rise to their challenge more successfully if they were aware that it is possible to lose weight by forgetting about losing weight. The better choice would be to examine their inner story and work out how to get the thoughts and feelings that will enable them to improve their physical wellbeing or view of self. They could also focus on the feelings or moods that are influencing their body confidence and their behaviour. They could reflect on how they could improve their emotional wellbeing too.

If you want to be happier forget about happiness, focus on your feelings and start lifting your mood. This will help you to alter your perspective on what is happening in your life. How you feel about an experience changes the experience. If you look at an experience in a different way the experience becomes different. Lift your mood and once you have lifted your mood in one area, just keep lifting elsewhere.

You will notice how you can feel and become happier. You will also notice how happiness spreads inside and outside of your mind. Happiness, like enthusiasm, is contagious.

The Short Story

Almost all of your happiness is constructed inside your mind.

How you interpret your world has the biggest influence on your happiness.

Perception is not reality.

Forgetting about happiness can make you happier.

Non-anger management can make you happier.

Focusing on the present can make you happier.

Being kind to your self and others can make you happier.

Life contains impermanence, complexity, injustice, pain and suffering.

You can learn how to lift your mood.

A happier life is more achievable than the happy life.

Chapter Eight
Being More Confident

When confidence begins it is invisible but it does not stay that way. Confidence starts inside a person's mind but we can sense when a person feels confident and we can also see confidence in the way that a person behaves. We can see it in individuals and we can also see it in groups and teams. This makes confidence appear to be mysterious but the good news is that confidence is fundamentally quite simple. To feel and be more confident you have to be the sort of person who trusts in your self.

In this chapter I will, amongst other things, encourage you to get out of your mind, teach you how to play the saxophone, explain why talking to your self is not the first sign of madness and offer you a free pass into the most exciting theme park in the world. In chapter one I explained how you create your unconscious mind and this chapter will take you deeper, giving you the opportunity to understand the content of your unconscious mind and how to access it. By the end of this chapter you will have an understanding of the essence of confidence and will be the sort of person who is more confident in a range of situations, including giving speeches or presentations in public.

But first of all, let's deal with the issue of self-trust.

Trust Your Self

To be confident, you have to trust that you will achieve what you want to achieve at a particular time, in a particular place and in a particular context. This includes those times when you have to step out of your comfort zone and those times when you take a leap of faith. You have to trust that you are the sort of person who will have a go, who will give their best to get to where they want to be and will do so despite the unexpected events, feelings or experiences that might emerge along the way. You have to trust that you will be able to combat your negative and closed inner voice when it tells you that the last person on earth that you should place your trust in is you.

The context for your confidence will vary according to the sort of person that you think you are and what your needs are. You might want to be more confident in your personal and professional relationships, it could be that you want more confidence in a competitive environment where you are up against an opponent whilst thousands of people are watching you, some for you and some against you, or you might need to be more confident in a situation where you are required to give a speech or a presentation in public. Maybe you want to become a little more confident in relation to your current confidence levels. These are all situations where you want your positive and open inner voice to replenish and reinforce your confidence.

Whatever your context, being confident means that you can rely on your self to be successful even if the unexpected happens and obstacles are placed in your way. The barriers to success that you need to overcome may be in your mind or they may be outside of your mind. The praise and compliments of others may help you to feel confident but ultimately confidence is down to your inner story, your view of self and your ability to trust in your self. Confidence is about you understanding your mind and placing full trust in your self. You have to be assured that once you decide to trust your self you can rely on your self to take on whatever your challenge is. Confidence relates to being self-assured as well as self-reliant. To trust your self you also have to talk to your self, more of that later.

To trust your self you have to believe in your self, but how do you do that?

Believe in your self
Trusting your self depends upon believing in your self. Self-belief and self-trust go hand in hand and this is where it gets less simple because, to have self-belief, there is more psychological work to be done.

Firstly you have to investigate your inner story. You have to examine the sense of 'Me' or 'I' that is created inside your head and the current beliefs that you hold true about who you think you are and what it means to be you. Self-belief is grounded in such thoughts: the thoughts that determine what you think you can and cannot do. Remember that thoughts and feelings exist in your unconscious as well as your conscious mind. Those residing in your unconscious mind are always there, ready and waiting for you to bring them to conscious awareness. It is the same for self-belief. Self-belief is conscious as well as unconscious – it exists even when you are not focusing on it. When you are aware of this you realise that self-belief needs nurturing and protecting. One of the reasons is that self-belief has the habit of wanting to be attached to outcomes and results and this can make it vulnerable and exposed when outcomes do not go as you want them to. Another reason is that there may be times when belief is just about you and your mind and if you do not believe in your self then who will? Helping your mind to focus on the process more than the outcome will provide greater opportunities for nurturing your self-belief.

Your confidence is highly dependent on your inner story. For many people it is rooted in the strand of their inner story that relates to their outer facing self. When they change their inner story and start to see 'self' differently they can begin to become more confident. The behaviour and words of others can also increase your confidence but the birthplace of confidence is your mind; that is where confidence begins. Therefore, understanding your mind will help you to learn to be more confident and change your world. For example, as emotions are constantly moving in your mind, if you attempt one thing that will make you feel more confident you can take advantage of the fluid nature of confidence and bring the confidence across from one area to boost your confidence in another. You can learn to be more confident because confidence moves; it is not a fixed emotional state.

Nurturing your self-belief enables it to become more robust. You can do this by encouraging your mind to be a collector of positive mental reminders. Doing so informs and reminds you that you can rely on your self to take the bold steps that will help you to attempt whatever task you set for your self or others set for you. Collect positive reminders by reflecting on previous success and storing up positive thoughts about your achievements. When you recognise, record and lock those positive thoughts and examples into your mind they become part of your inner story. Anything that illustrates and demonstrates that you are moving one step nearer to becoming more confident has to be recognised and validated in your mind so that you can increase your trust in your self and in your capacity to succeed. A positive thought, like a sincere apology, can travel a long way

How Confidence Works Inside The Mind

Recently I was speaking at a conference. It was not a large audience: there were approximately five hundred people attending. I had one hour for my keynote presentation and the event organiser had requested that I forward the slides that accompanied my talk in advance. I agreed to do this; there were only six slides so it was easy for me to meet my deadline.

On the day of the presentation, I arrived with ten minutes to go before the start of the event, much later than I had planned. This was due to a traffic incident involving a dog with a distorted concept of self, a motorcyclist with non-anger management issues and a tent pole. That is a long and convoluted story so it is probably best kept for another time. The event organiser hastily greeted me at the door, breathing and speaking rapidly. I assumed that he had been caught up in the same traffic delay too but I was wrong. There was a localised electricity problem in the building and I was not going to be able to use my slides. His angst was audible, palpable and working overtime in its desire to be projected onto me. I explained to him that what he was experiencing as a problem in his world was not a problem in my world. I also expressed my view that a slide-free presentation might be a welcome relief for the audience members. For some people who are about to speak in public, turning up to a conference and finding that you are unable to rely on your slides would exist on a continuum ranging from problematic to disastrous, but this is not the case for me. Why? Because of the way confidence works inside my mind.

I trust myself and I believe in myself to be successful in such situations. Why wouldn't I? I knew what I wanted to talk about and I had prepared well, including how I was going to structure the pace and content of my presentation. I knew where the key signposts were and at what points I wanted to interact with the audience. I also knew at what points they might want to interact with me. The slides contained a few key words and some relevant visual images. They were intended to embed a message or to prompt reflection and therefore my only real challenge would be to think on my feet about doing that differently. I was there to interact with the audience and I was not there to interact with the slides. There was no need to frame the situation as a problem. That is a description of what was going on in my mind.

He looked at me as if I had just landed in his world from another planet as I rubbed my hands together, smiled, asked him to notice how relaxed I was – so that I could calm him down – and I asked him if we could get underway. I began the presentation trusting my self to present well, to enjoy the next hour and to have fun. That's how confidence works. You have to believe in your self and trust in your self. The more you trust your self the less tense and more liberated you feel, the higher your expectations and aspirations will become and the more confidence you gain. I paid attention to the open voice in my head that was telling me that I enjoy unpredictability. I had no intention of paying attention to the closed voice inside my mind. The voice that would love to tell me, if I allowed it to, that situations like this are a disaster and it will be downhill all the way for the next hour that will, assisted by the time distortion that anxiety creates, feel like a hand-trembling lifetime. My self-belief belongs to me and your self-belief belongs to you. Self-belief cannot be left unattended. It likes to be nurtured so that it can grow and your open inner voice is the voice that enables it to do so. Self-belief enables you to become more confident and more competent.

The Best Confidence

Before I continue I want to clarify what type of confidence I believe is the best confidence for your inner story. I believe that robust confidence is sustained by humility. Your mind can be bursting at the seams with confidence and self-belief but it is vital that you always remain grounded and humble. Confidence without humility will breed overconfidence and arrogance. In some elite sport settings there are people whose self-belief and self-trust is so solid that when they perform they can be perceived as being arrogant. This is how they may appear as a performer but when you know them as people they are often grounded and humble. There is a difference between arrogance as a way of performing and arrogance as a way of being.

And Breathe

Soon we shall consider psychological strategies that can help you to be more confident as a public speaker. Before we do that I would like to pass on some advice that I was given that can be applied generally to situations where confidence is critical. As a young saxophone player my teacher used to tell me that playing the saxophone was not about technical ability because "everyone of a certain level can do all of the fast-fingers stuff". His view was that to play the saxophone you had to learn about your diaphragm and get to know your diaphragm. He often said,

> "To play the saxophone you have to know how to breathe.
> That's what makes a great saxophone player."

His argument was that as a person progresses through the technical levels they should learn how to breathe differently and become better at breathing because this allows you to feel the music rather than just play it. His belief was that your fingers will learn to do all of the technical work but it is diaphragm control that creates the tone of the instrument and allows you to connect with the music. "It is all about controlling your breathing" was his advice. He was right. As those people who spend time learning how to control their breathing know, your breathing and your emotions are mysteriously connected. That is why, when people learn how to breathe deeply and really focus on their breathing for the first time, they often find that they burst into tears or find themselves laughing uncontrollably or both. The quality of your breathing control enables you to be relaxed enough for your unconscious mind to execute the more challenging aspects of the technical work. Many things in life are uncontrollable but you can control your breathing. Learning to do so keeps you relaxed and allows you to perform better, it makes you feel calm and composed and as a consequence it enables you to be present in the moment and trust in your self.

Before you attempt any task where you need to be more confident begin it by pretending that you are about to play the saxophone.

Now let's look in a practical way at a specific context for being more confident – public speaking. In chapter five you read about how fear flows in your mind and this is highly relevant for people who are frightened of public speaking.

Here, I am going to focus more on the anxiety that people have about public speaking and how that type of anxiety can be replaced by confidence. After that we will move on from the psychology of talking to others to the psychology of talking to your self.

Be More Confident at Public Speaking

I have often heard it said that surveys indicate that, in some countries, people's anxiety about public speaking is greater than it is about their own death. It has been an unsuccessful endeavour on my part to find a valid evidence base for this claim. It may be an urban myth or it may be a claim that is based upon reliable and valid research. Whether there is evidence for this claim or not, I have met many people who have anxieties about speaking to groups in public either at work or outside of the work context.

Naturally, anxieties that people have about standing up in front of others to speak will relate to their inner story, especially to their outer-facing self. Being comfortable with your sense of public self and the attention that others might pay to it when you speak reduces your anxiety levels and increases your composure when you speak in public. However, there are clearly many people who do not occupy that particular psychological space and the mere thought of speaking in front of ten people can be as terrifying to them as talking in front of one thousand. So, what can you do to help you be more confident when speaking in public? How can your mind help you become more confident in this situation?

Here are a few questions to consider as you explore how to be a more confident public speaker.

What if public speaking was nothing to do with your public self at all? How would you feel about it then? What would happen if you placed more focus on the audience and on the content of what you say than on your own self? What if you could remove your anxiety about feeling that you are being judged as a person – even though the audience is not really doing that? What if you could remove your anxiety about having every word you say critically analysed and dissected – even though the audience is not really doing that either? What if you could shrink your anxiety to the point that it disappears?

How would you feel about speaking in public then?

Of course, you may not be the sort of person who dreads public speaking; you may already be confident but want to be more confident. If you have any anxieties at all about public speaking it is useful to consider what is going on inside your head *before* you even speak in public, as this will tell your brain what to look for when you are speaking in public. If you want to win you have to prepare to win. If you want to speak well in public you have to prepare to speak well in public. Remember too that whatever you focus on expands. This means that you have to focus on the right thing and that is not your own anxiety. Being able to shrink the significance of anything that makes you anxious is a skill that you can learn and develop.

Notice the pattern

Inside your head your brain is always searching for patterns from which it can make meaning. Being conscious that patterning is happening inside your head can help to reduce anxiety before and during public speaking. When you are anxious you become more suggestible and you can begin to pay attention to the wrong things. Anxiety influences patterning and if you are not in control of patterning when you are speaking in public your brain may make matters worse for you. For example, it may reveal to you the one face that stands out amongst the crowd that appears to be disappointed or disinterested – just like it can help a member of a band notice the one person who is not dancing or a comedian notice the one person who is not laughing.

I am not suggesting here that you can always tell what people are thinking or feeling by interpreting their facial expressions, a practice made even more complex by cultural nuances. I am referring to what the process of patterning can cause you to pay attention to, when it could also help you to focus on the many interested faces in your audience instead.

The patterning process is always active. When speaking in public it can present thoughts or stories to you that suddenly appear from your unconscious to your conscious mind and invite you to respond impulsively and say them aloud. Some may be helpful but some may not. You have to be in touch with your own patterning before and throughout your presentation otherwise you may find that you consistently respond to emerging thoughts. Once you are aware of your own patterning, you realise that the brain of every audience member will be patterning too. Being conscious of this helps you to focus on how you will get your message across to them. Thinking about how the audience patterns can help you to ensure that they make the right meaning, the meaning you want them to make, out of what they are seeing, hearing and experiencing.

Meet needs

Before you speak in public it is important to identify the needs of the audience, even if you have never met them before, so that the content of your presentation matches their needs. Be clear in your mind about why they are there and what you want them to pay attention to during and after your presentation – and that includes their feelings as well as their thoughts. This will help you to meet their needs. Thinking in this way immediately takes the focus onto what you can control: your presentation. It also makes you think less about you being the centre of attention, or about people judging you, and places your focus more on your audience than it does on you. You are now thinking about them and how to guide them to focus on the right thing. The language that you use to direct their attention helps here.

"I am pleased to be with you today to talk about..."
"As you will notice here..."
"As you pay attention now to..."
"To remind you of the key points that matter..."
"Thank you for your time and attention..."

There is a big difference between hearing and listening. We all hear and listen in different ways. When you talk to a group you want to ensure that they are hearing what you say but to meet their needs you also have to think about what it is you want them to listen to. Focusing on what you are going to say, and the messages that you are going to convey during your presentation, lecture, pitch or speech increases the structure and clarity of your communication. Everyone in your audience will be patterning in unique and different ways. This is why it is important to vary the pace, space, tone and content of your presentation. These are some of the components of the scaffolding of your presentation that will allow you to build audience understanding of what you are saying and engage their attention in different ways. You also need scaffolding because when you are in full flow you will not be paying conscious attention to every word you are saying.

Your unconscious mind will be helping you by recognising where you are in the progressive phases of your presentation and recognising what you had rehearsed earlier. Your presentation may flow smoothly but this will be because your unconscious mind will be behaving like the furious feet of a duck, paddling energetically under the water, while the body gracefully glides along the surface. Turning up at a venue and giving a presentation that has minimal structure and is essentially off-the-cuff may work occasionally but meeting the needs of your audience consistently requires paying attention to the structure and scaffolding of your presentation. The art of presenting is not only about your ability to perform.

Emotions love to move inside your head. When you speak in public you need to remember that they also move outside of your head too. If you are feeling anxious you can transmit your anxiety to your audience and cause them to become anxious too. If you do this, both you and your audience are focusing on the wrong thing:

you are feeling anxious about your presentation going well and, unfortunately for you, so are they.

Think alongside

Public speaking is like business coaching or teaching in that, in your mind, it should be more about 'being alongside' than it is about 'being in front of'. A teacher who believes that teaching is solely about being in front of the learners can fall swiftly into the trap of being too didactic. All learning needs cannot be met this way. A business coach who thinks that coaching is about being in front of their client can fall into the trap of thinking that listening is not about understanding or making authentic connection but is about waiting for your turn to speak. The needs of clients cannot be met this way.

When you speak in public you are usually standing in front of a group and often on an elevated platform or raised stage. Psychologically, the physical elevation of someone or something makes a visible statement about both status and significance. You can observe this principle in sacred spaces where spiritual teachings are disseminated from lecterns and pulpits while the congregation physically and metaphorically look up towards the person who is delivering or interpreting the scripture. Hindu deities and the holy books of many faiths are afforded the respect of being placed on raised platforms. When you speak in public it is likely that you will be in an elevated position on a platform, just like actors, musicians and politicians often are. It is also likely that you will be physically in front of your audience. Even if you are not on a platform it is likely that you will be standing up and they will be sitting down. Where you are in terms of the physical space could entice you to pattern in a way that amplifies your significance. It is easy for a power dynamic to come into play here and the inside of your mind can trick you into thinking that it is all about you. A person engaging in public speaking who thinks it is about being in front of their audience can fall into the trap of thinking that this situation is all about 'Me' and not about 'Them'. The needs of the audience cannot be met in this way.

Although you may be physically in front of a group of people it will always work better for them, and for you, if you think about it in your mind as working *alongside* them rather than in front of them. This reduces your anxiety and increases your ability to engage with the audience.

Engage with your audience

Engaging with the audience is one of the key characteristics of the craft and art of any successful presentation. If you feel anxious, engaging with the audience right from the start of your presentation deflects your attention away from your self, thereby reducing your anxiety. Remember the value of humour, but not necessarily jokes, in the way that it helps people to feel engaged and at ease too. Psychologically, the audience wants to know that everything is going to be fine and humour is one way of helping them to relax. Engaging with the audience does not have to mean direct interaction and participation with them. Engaging can also mean being conscious of how you will support them in following the flow of your presentation so that they can make meaning out of your message. Engaging with the audience will prevent the occurrence of one of the major drivers of anxiety when speaking in public: being in awe of your audience.

For some presenters this can simply relate to how many people are in the audience. For others it can relate to who is present in the audience. If you are anxious about public speaking pay attention to the spelling rather than the sound of the word 'audience'. There may be a reason why it is not spelt 'awedience'. As performers and musicians know, the audience is there to listen to you and you can create a mutual connection when they do so. You will want to thank them for their attention and participation too but they are not there for you to be in awe of them.

Play the game not the occasion

Finally, you can also learn to be a better and more confident public speaker by reflecting on how some performers in sport control what their mind should and should not pay attention to before they compete in big events. They often arrive early at a stadium, especially if it is a stadium that they have not competed at before.

You will have seen some teams walk out onto a pitch before a game. Some players like to inspect the pitch; some will stand on the pitch and create moving mental images in their mind so that they can visualise playing and performing well. Others will absorb the atmosphere to enable them to relax into it. Doing this also helps them to create a sense of perspective by shrinking the significance of the occasion.

This type of behaviour is important because to perform well you have to be both energised and relaxed at the same time. You cannot afford to become caught up in the emotional pressure that can surround a big event because you need to trust your self and believe in your ability to respond and perform when it matters. Nor can you afford to be distracted by the atmosphere when you perform. In other words, when top performers prepare in this way they are making sure that before they compete and when they compete they play the game and not the occasion.

Your performance can be influenced by *pressure* and *stress*. Some people thrive under pressure, they love pressure, but they are the people who know their inner story and can differentiate between what pressure and stress mean to them in their world. Some elite performers thrive under pressure because they know the point at which pressure becomes stress for them: when the demands stop being challenging and start to become overwhelming. It is impossible to relax when you feel overwhelmed because whatever it is that stresses you will prevent you from thinking with clarity and focusing on the right thing. Psychologically you need to ensure that pressure, where you feel you can respond positively and creatively to a situation, does not turn into stress where you feel that you do not have the mental resources to be able to cope.

When performers appear unable to handle pressure it is often described as 'cracking under pressure' or 'choking under pressure' but this is not really an accurate description of what is happening in the mind. It is actually the moment of conversion in their mind at which pressure turns into stress that they are struggling to deal with. It is that split second when they have to dig deep and find the mental toughness and emotional resources to be the best they can be. That moment of conversion from pressure to stress is highly individual and it is always beneficial to understand your mind so that you can establish what it looks like for you. People crack under stress and choke under stress. It is the stress that gets to them not the pressure.

If you are anxious about public speaking reduce your anxiety by arriving early at the venue where you are giving your presentation. You can also learn from the behaviour of female and male actors. There are times when an individual will go onto the stage in an empty theatre to warm up vocally in the environment in which they are about to perform. There are times when a whole theatre company will do this together inside the empty theatre where they will soon be performing. You can do something similar by rehearsing parts or all of your presentation out loud in the room while nobody else is present. This will reduce the potential stress of the situation; it will help you to focus on the game not the occasion and will also have the added benefit of warming your voice up.

If you are already in the room and are about to present to a small group you can welcome each person with a handshake as they arrive. This creates a sense of hospitality and warmth rather than the sense of detachment that can occur in a context where the audience has come to listen to an 'expert'. A presenter can still offer expertise but it does not have to feel to the audience as if it is being imparted within a hierarchical or potentially patronising dynamic. Welcoming the audience as they arrive gives them the sense that you are inviting them into your space, a space where you are relaxed and comfortable. It feels good when you arrive as a member of an audience and notice that a speaker is very happy to be there. You infer that they are self-assured and confident and, as a consequence, you anticipate that all will go well.

Another way of playing the game and not the occasion is to focus on the content of your presentation more than the context for your presentation. Focusing on the content allows you to be more composed and confident. It enables you to perform at your best. It takes your focus away from your public self. The audience will not be scrutinising every word you say, every move you make and every item you are wearing. They will be making an initially unconscious emotional connection with you, and although you have not stopped your presentation to give everyone a hug, they will be making unconscious judgments about your warmth as a person. They will also be making judgments about your competence. The warmth and competence evaluators of the audience members are always on alert in the first moments of interacting with someone who is giving a presentation. This will be happening if they meet a presenter before the formality of the presentation starts. Ensuring that the content of your talk meets the needs of the audience helps to inform their perception of your competence. Engagement with the audience as individuals or as a whole group helps to inform their perception of your warmth.

We have seen how important your unconscious mind is in relation to your confidence. Now we shall start to look further at how confidence works within your mind so that you can access it when you need to. Let's take a deep dive and explore what is happening in your mind. We will focus mainly on your unconscious mind, which is most of your mind, and see how you can gain access to it.

Understand Your Unconscious Mind

You already know that your conscious mind contains what you are currently aware of and your unconscious mind contains what you are currently unaware of. Exploring your unconscious mind is like spending time visiting the most wonderfully sophisticated theme park that you could ever possibly imagine – a theme park of hidden complexity and surprises that are not currently conscious. Your unconscious mind is the best theme park in the world and not only because it helps to construct the 'emotional rollercoaster' that is much loved by those who describe volatile emotional experiences.

Your unconscious mind influences your motivations, values, beliefs, intuition, judgments, feelings and potentials. It influences your physiology. It is possible to have a nightmare and wake up sweating or shouting. Your pulse is racing, your breathing rate is in superfast mode and you might even be physically shaking too. Consciously this might appear to be an extreme reaction when nothing has really happened. Except it has. You are encountering a physical response to an experience that you were convinced was taking place in real time in the real world. Your unconscious mind is phenomenally powerful. Imagine what it would be like if you could access those thoughts in your unconscious mind that are restricting your confidence right now. Imagine what it would be like if you could access those thoughts and change them. You know, those thoughts that create pervasive self-doubt and enjoy convincing you to remain firmly within your comfort zone.

Imagine what it would be like if you could do that. Well, you already know how to do it. There will have been times when you have needed to access hidden information in your unconscious mind so that it can be made known to you. For example, think about a time when you tried to remember a name of someone you met years ago or maybe a place, a book or a song title and said,

"I will get it in a moment, it's on the tip of my tongue."

After a few attempts you somehow mysteriously find the name. However, it was not sitting there right on the tip of your tongue waiting to be spoken. You were on a rapid search through your unconscious mind where the answer was located and your unconscious mind helped you to find the answer.

The content of your unconscious mind

It has long been a matter of interest and investigation as to whether it is possible to know what is stored in the unconscious mind. Body language experts propose that from your face all the way down to your feet you are constantly giving off non-verbal signals called 'tells'. It is claimed that 'tells' are unconscious behaviours that offer an insight into your unconscious attitudes, thoughts and feelings. Some 'tells' appear to be obvious to the observer, such as the incongruence between what you communicate verbally and what your body is communicating.

I was once involved in a conversation where people began to talk about their careers and speak about their favourite jobs. A member of the military began to talk about how he loved serving his country and what a privilege it was to do so. Someone then informed the group about how much she had enjoyed her time serving in the military too. She said it was the best job that she had ever had. I found this statement confusing as she had previously been talking about how much she had enjoyed working in an environment that was radically different and she appeared to be more energised and enthusiastic when doing so. I was curious. I asked politely if she was sure that working in the military had really been her best job. She replied with a mildly unconvincing "yes" while her head, instead of nodding up and down to affirm what she was saying, moved from one side to another to indicate "no". The 'tell' was clear. The incongruence was evident. The mismatch was revealing. Other less obvious tells require forensic levels of micro-moment, micro-expression and micro-signal analysis to discern what is really being communicated.

Dreamworld

When you are in a wakeful state your conscious mind is active. When you are sleeping you have no external stimulus to focus on; your muscles relax, your eyes are closed and there comes a time when you are no longer awake. You do not completely lose consciousness; it is best to think about it as your unconscious mind taking over the controls for a while. This is the time when you are likely to dream and therefore explains why some psychologists and therapists see dreams as a gateway to the content of the unconscious mind. Once you have been asleep for some time you may begin to have vivid dreams and in dreamworld anything is possible. Certain dream analysts propose that dreams offer insight into your own latent thoughts, emotions, tensions, experiences, wishes, preoccupations and fantasies that spend their time repressed within the unconscious mind. Dreams are seen as allowing you to become acquainted with the contents of your unconscious mind and helping you to find answers and solutions to life's challenges.

Other dream analysts propose that a dream is a space where every person you meet and every image that you encounter is a deeper representation of characteristics of your self that your unconscious mind is processing on your behalf.

There are times when your conscious mind takes time to process whether something happened in the real world or if it took place in dreamworld. Research illustrates that when people dream that their 'significant other' has been behaving in an unfaithful way, the relationship can become more problematic the following morning. The dreamer wakes up feeling irrationally suspicious, and the potential for conflict with their partner in the first waking hours increases. Again, nothing has really happened. Except it has. I also acknowledge that there are those who believe that dreams have no meaning or function at all and are simply a form of mental delirium that can occur when you are not awake.

There are many ways of gaining access to your unconscious mind. My preference is to make this process speedier and easier by encouraging you to 'get out of your mind' rather than to suggest that you spend years engaged in analysis or dream therapy. By championing the process of getting out of your mind I am not recommending that you do anything illegal. You can get out of your mind by tapping into a legal and common human experience that still remains an under-used resource.

Talking to Yourself Means You Are Out of Your Mind

A popular phrase insists that talking to your self is the first sign of madness. This notion emerges from the days when many forms of mental illness were generally referred to as 'madness' and when 'talking to yourself' was a description of audible visual hallucinations. If you are the sort of person who talks to your self, I am not about to advise that you should stop participating in this activity, far from it. Talking to yourself is not the first sign of madness but I do have to tell you that talking to your self does mean that you are out of your mind.

Being out of your mind is a great place to be, especially if you want to be more confident.

Self-talk matters

I have already described many of the advantages of paying attention to your positive inner voice. So let's bring your inner voice back into focus now. Stop for a moment, become conscious of it, be silent and take some time to listen to it. It may not be coincidental that 'listen' is an anagram of 'silent'. Be silent and listen to it again. When you have listened once in any situation it is always useful to listen again. You may begin to notice that what you say to your self inside your mind really matters. It can have an impact on your sense of who you are, your confidence and on your performance.

In terms of impact on performance, the field of sport psychology heralds the inherent value of self-talk in relation to inspirational and motivational aspects of achieving high performance. This makes a lot of sense because, for example, in a professional tennis game you might have to talk to your self for over four hours without any intervention from a coach. At times like this, the voice inside your mind may need to keep reminding you that you have earned the right to be where you are and that one of the reasons you play your sport is because you have an unwavering belief in your ability to win. Your positive inner voice can remind you that you are fearless and ruthless in competition when you need to be and reinforce that you compete at your best when the pressure is intense. Your inner voice will reinforce that you are the sort of person who thrives and wins when the mental and physical conditions make extreme demands on you and your opponent.

Self-speak matters more

Self-talk is clearly a positive strategy but it is not enough because self-talk means that you stay inside your mind. The major issue here is that there is still an astonishing amount of activity going on in your mind when you are talking to your self. When you self-talk you still have to encourage your mind to pay full attention to your inner voice because there are many distractions racing around doing their best to gain your attention. My preference is to encourage people to increase awareness of their inner voice by engaging in 'self-speak'– articulating out loud what they hear their inner-voice saying. Self-speaking allows you to become aware of what is emerging from your unconscious to your conscious mind and to pay full attention to it.

The process is similar to what might happen when someone stops us in the street and asks for directions from one place to another. We visualise the route that the person needs to take and describe how to get there, often accompanying our explanation with gestures; we spontaneously draw a map for them by waving our arms around in the air. What we are doing here is taking something visual from our mind and externalising it in a visual form. When we self-speak we take something auditory from our mind and externalise it in an auditory form.

When you self-speak you are no longer inside your mind, you are out of your mind. The term 'out of your mind' has connotations associated with being in a psychological state that is completely uncontaminated by thinking. I use the term differently. When you are out of your mind your thoughts are externalised; you are thinking out loud. Being out of your mind allows you to become far more aware of what is going on in your mind. For example, in the privacy of a dressing room, a locker room or a changing room there are people who take time to look in a mirror and self-speak before they go out to perform,

"Come on, you will do it."
"This is your moment."
"Give everything you've got."

They do this to reinforce positive thoughts and expectations that are already in their mind. Remember, if you expect it to happen you allow it to happen. They also do this to focus on the right thing and reinforce self-trust.

There are many benefits of talking out loud to your self. Talking aloud can sometimes help you when you are searching for something that you have recently lost. I'm not suggesting that you start wandering about in public loudly exclaiming,

"My dignity."
"My integrity."
"My self-respect."

I am referring to situations where you have mislaid items such as your keys, your phone or your glasses. Walking around saying "keys, keys, keys" helps you to find your keys as it can help your brain to pattern for them and focus on the right thing. You may have had the experience of walking from one room to another and saying aloud,

"What did I come into this room for?"

Having articulated the question your unconscious mind intuitively helps you to find the answer.

Research shows that self-speaking is good for your memory and therefore it can help when you are rehearsing for a presentation or pitch, preparing for an examination or learning your lines in a script. Talking out loud to your self can help you to figure out a solution to a problem. Sometimes, talking out loud to another person can help you to figure out a solution even if they do not respond to you. Self-speak can also help you to remain structured if you use it to prepare for a conversation where you have to assert your point of view to a person more senior than you in a hierarchy, such as a boss or a team leader. Self-speak might also help you to find items as you walk in a supermarket, although, as you will see later, other factors outside of your control might impact on your success in this situation.

A Chronic People-Pleaser Learns How to Say No

Imagine what it must feel like if you lack the confidence to say "no" to people even though you would desperately like to. Maybe you do not have to imagine because you already experience this feeling? Perhaps you are the sort of person who experiences this feeling with some people but not with others? I'd like to introduce you to Maria. I met Maria because she had become a chronic people-pleaser. No matter how unmanageable her life became she just could not say "no". She would always say "yes" despite the stress and logistical difficulties that saying "yes" consistently caused for her. When I explored Maria's inner story with her I was interested to discover that Maria was the daughter of an alcoholic.

Here you will see the links between her life story and her inner story and how self-speaking raised her confidence. Maria was the eldest child of a reliably unreliable father. She told me that as far back as she was able to remember she always felt that as the eldest child she had to "make things right", especially for her mum. Maria was the bearer of a self-generated burden of responsibility even at the age of ten years old. She felt responsible for intervening when her father returned home after he had been drinking because she knew he could behave aggressively. Maria believed that her father would not hit his wife in front of their only child. Sometimes Maria would sneak out of bed without her mum knowing and remain at the top of the stairs on sentry duty, listening out for her father's night-time return.

Maria's inner story became generalised as she moved through her teenage years and into adulthood. "I am the sort of person who makes things right for my mother" altered into "I am the sort of person who makes things right for others". This was all happening unconsciously and by the time Maria was an adult it had developed into, "I am the sort of person who is unable to say no".

In her own words, Maria had "turned into an out of control people-pleaser". Her people-pleasing antennae were so active that she could sense a problem emerging when it was a substantial distance away and would respond habitually and unconsciously. Before she knew it she was on the scene in no time at all offering help or agreeing to requests for help. It had all gone too far and it was devouring her time and energy in both her personal and professional life. It was also damaging her confidence because she wanted to behave differently but felt helpless about being able to do so.

The solution was for Maria to change her inner story radically and quickly. Asking Maria to go from saying "yes" to saying "no", when it was appropriate for her to do so, was too much of a leap even though that is what she wanted to do. It is the same difficulty as trying to go from unhappy to happy or angry to calm. Initially we worked together to lift her confidence to the point that she trusted herself to be able to turn down the incessant requests for her time and to control the persistent desire to want to make things right for others. It is difficult to say "no" when saying "yes" has become a learned behaviour that you now need to unlearn. Therefore, we searched for another option; a phrase whose underlying message was "no" but was much easier for Maria to say than "no". One strategy we employed was to introduce a phrase that changed the emphasis from the outcome of saying "no" to the process of saying "no". The bottom line here is that there is no value in having a phrase to apply to a situation unless you actually have the confidence to say it. Maria told me how self-speaking this phrase when she was on her own empowered her. The more she heard it aloud the more she became used to hearing it and this eventually gave her the courage to say it in situations when it was appropriate to do so. Her variation on saying "no" was,

"I am sorry, I can't give my full attention to that right now."

This phrase worked very well for her. Most people are not rude enough to retort, "when can you give your full attention to what I'm asking you to do?" If anyone did say something that resembled this type of response Maria had a plan up her sleeve and would offer a time that seemed to be a long way off. The intention of this strategy was to challenge the person making the request to think about how urgent their need was. If someone says they cannot give their full attention to your request now, then you are forced to consider the urgency of your need.

A simple phrase self-spoken before it was applied altered her ability to begin to take control of her time, energy and most importantly her inner story. Self-speaking helped Maria to get to a more confident place and she became empowered to say "no". Maria's confidence in one area of her life began to spread to other areas.

Stay Conscious in the Supermarket

I was in a supermarket last Christmas. Supermarkets are notorious environments for doing all they can to influence your unconscious mind. There is a multisensory greeting when you enter followed by meticulously planned product placement. Then, when you have finished negotiating the thin aisles that deliberately slow down human traffic to encourage you to pay attention to products placed at eye level, you arrive at the checkout to see chocolates and sweets winking at you as they signal a well-earned reward at the end of your onerous task. As a consequence of being aware of this, I always enter a supermarket with my conscious mind in full control. Conscious shopping is far less costly than the unconscious version.

Just after my arrival, above the gentle, warm lulling of Christmas music, I could hear a man behind me chanting, "cloves, cloves, cloves".

Such behaviour might cause other shoppers to offer him a wide berth but to me it was not only compelling it was also particularly impressive. He appeared to be using repetitive self-speaking to keep his conscious mind focused on finding the spice collection. Unfortunately, an assistant approached him and brought his mesmerising incantation to an abrupt halt.

"Cloves, cloves, cloves."
"Can I help you, sir?"
"Yes please, I'm making mulled wine and looking for cloves."
"No problem, sir. Let me take you to the correct aisle."

Without further ado, the assistant led him towards the section that contained the shirts, jumpers and trousers.

The Short Story

Confidence is rooted in your inner story.

Confidence is fluid.

It is possible to learn how to be more confident, especially at speaking in public.

Self-belief exists even when you are not thinking about it.

Play the game not the occasion.

If you talk aloud to your self you are out of your mind.

If you expect it to happen you allow it to happen.

Visit the best theme park in the world.

Self-talking is good, self-speaking is better.

Trust your self.

Chapter Nine
Being A Better Leader

Leadership is an expression of your inner story. That is why leaders can be open, humble and respectful and still lead teams that perform and deliver. It is why leaders can feign modesty, have overly favourable views of their leadership competence and never accept that they are part of the problem when everyone else can see that they are. It is also why leaders can have a personal need to generate chaos and crisis so that they can impress everyone by becoming the captain of the lifeboat. Your inner story determines the essence of leadership and what leadership means to you.

In this chapter I will, amongst other things, show you how you can make a miracle happen overnight, warn you to be on guard after someone tickles you under the chin, explain why the size of your shoes impacts upon your ability to lead and explain why you are exactly the same as everyone else, similar to some other people and completely unique.

You will read about how leaders can identify and meet the needs of every member of their team. I will also introduce you to epoché: this is the strand of an inner story that, if it is missing, will prevent you from developing empathy. We will also explore the relationship between leadership and coaching and the chapter concludes with two beautiful questions. Leadership begins inside your mind and so do similar concepts like coaching, teaching and parenting. Whilst the context for this chapter is to help you become the sort of person who is a better leader, it could apply to being a better coach and certain aspects do apply to being a better teacher or parent.

One Size Fits Nobody

I will not be delving into theories of leadership nor will I be offering any flat-pack better-leader templates. Theories and templates are not specific to *you* and what is happening in your mind, so they

172

do not appear here. Also, there can be a huge gap between theory and reality. An academic theory may appear to be beautiful but once it has been tested the real world evidence to support it can sometimes make it far less attractive. There are even times when getting something done and asking afterwards, "does this work in theory?" is a much better option than procrastinating while you analyse whether a theory will work in practice. This is not a chapter about leadership theories.

There are many psychometric tests that claim to tell you what type of leader you are or what type of leader you can be in the future. This chapter will be avoiding those as well. The reason for this is that when you begin to consider how to become a better leader it is a highly individual and a highly personal process that depends upon a range of personal and environmental factors. Psychometric tests may be able to assist you in navigating somewhere towards understanding who you are. However, they are also more likely to indicate the sort of person that you, consciously or unconsciously, would like the psychometric test to tell you that you are: your ideal self with a glossily varnished veneer. Their one-size-fits-all approach means they are unable to get to the essence of who each individual is. Their outcomes are unable to identify what it means to be you. They mumble more than they speak.

This illuminates how their one-size-fits-all approach is really a one-size-fits-nobody approach. Knowing your inner story will get to the essence of who you are and help you to understand what it means to be you; psychometrics and paint-by-numbers personality testing will not and therefore they do not appear in this chapter either.

Leadership is About...

Because leadership is an expression of every person's inner story, leadership is about multiple aspects of inner stories. Here are some of those aspects:

Leadership is about who you are and what you stand for

Your followers must know the whole, honest and authentic you and be clear about your values and your expectations. Of course, you also need to know the whole authentic you too. This means knowing how your view of self affects your thoughts, feelings and actions.

Leadership is about relationships

You cannot be a leader without having followers and you cannot be a better leader without focusing on developing better relationships with those that you are leading, influencing and motivating. Your team has to understand you because their perceptions of you will have an impact upon their willingness to be led by you. For relationships to be meaningful, you need to understand the lived experience of those that you lead and be willing to listen, learn, adapt and respond. This influences their respect for you.

Leadership is about style

There are many styles of leadership available to you. You can be a transactional leader, you can be a transformational leader and it is also possible for someone to be given the title 'leader' within a system even though they demonstrate a complete absence of leadership qualities. Leaders can adopt a style where they model the behaviours and attitudes that they want from those they are leading thus demonstrating to their followers how to be and what to do. You can lead from the front if that is your preferred style or you can lead from the centre, which may ultimately work better for you. Some leaders choose to combine both approaches. However, it is difficult to lead from the back, even though you might know some leaders who adopt that approach.

Leadership is about being more conscious

Better leaders are more conscious of what their inner story is, in relation to leadership, so that they can establish what works better for them as a leader. Being conscious of your own inner story allows you to connect authentically with the inner story of others and establish an environment in which their story, and yours, can flourish. Better leaders are also conscious of what is emerging within them and around them, but more about that later.

Leadership is about being you – but with additional skills

Better leaders accept and embrace who they are. When you are fully accepting of who you are you can give your whole self to your leadership task. You can also consider what new leadership skills you need and what current skills you wish to develop in order to become a better leader. But where do you start? What skills do you need more of and what skills do you need to develop now?

Leadership Skills

There are many leadership skills. Some are social skills, some are performance skills and some are defined as 'soft' skills such as empathy, compassion and being sensitive to issues of wellbeing in the workplace and beyond. When you are changing your inner story in relation to leadership it is helpful to think of leadership skills in terms of the following three categories: technical skills, conceptual skills and people skills.

Technical skills

Leaders need to have knowledge about the technical skills that are important to specific activities that take place within the context in which they lead. They may well have excelled in these technical skills too. Technical knowledge will afford them credibility amongst their followers. Some leaders are promoted to their leadership position based solely upon their technical excellence. However, technical excellence is not enough to be a better leader. You need more than that. This may go some way towards explaining why some technically gifted football players have struggled to become high impact leaders when they become 'managers' of professional teams. Leadership is about much more than having technical skills and possessing technical knowledge, to be a better leader you need conceptual and people skills too.

Conceptual skills

Conceptual skills are psychological by nature. These skills will include being able to engage with and manipulate concepts and ideas as well as being capable of creating and implementing a vision and strategy. They include imagining, creating and developing a culture, being able to establish and model values and keeping a sense of perspective by seeing the bigger picture and taking a long view. Conceptual skills help you to problem-find as well as to problem-solve. Technical ability is not necessarily a reliable predictor of a person having a range of conceptual skills. Having a range of conceptual skills is not necessarily a reliable predictor of a leader having the required people skills either.

People skills

People skills are exactly what the label says they are. They place a spotlight on your humanity and how it is expressed in the way that you interact with people. People skills are vital in creating and enabling a culture of active rather than passive followership; a culture where people feel valued and respected and want to do what you are asking them to do rather that simply doing it because it has been requested. People skills include being able to create a sense of meaning and purpose, identifying and meeting needs, offering both motivational and developmental feedback and respecting diversity and difference. When a leader does this it makes individuals want to work collaboratively for the leader and for the team.

People skills also include knowing how inner stories shape the reality, shared meaning and performance of individuals and teams. They help a leader to create team engagement and to empower and encourage their team members to develop professionally and personally. People skills involve lifting and nurturing people as well as providing them with opportunities to learn and develop. Better leaders elevate as well as educate. People skills are also necessary to help you to understand and respond to the breadth of psychological responses that people can have towards leaders including admiration, respect, dependency, envy and resentment.

Leadership skills move up and down

What is interesting in thinking about these three categories of leadership skills is that you can see how skills move up and down according to the level of leadership involved. In large organisations, the more that you progress through the leadership hierarchy the more the need for people and conceptual skills increases and the need for technical skills decreases.

This helps us to understand why, when under pressure or when encountering leadership anxiety, some leaders dive back into the technical detail. If they are doing this to offer experience and support to the team then that is welcome by the team. If they are doing it for psychological reasons, such as ego inflation, to ward off status anxiety or for an injection of self-comfort and security then that will be irritating for the team. It also makes people in the team feel they are not trusted and therefore is as welcome as a snake in a sleeping bag. As a leader, reverting to the technical aspects of your role, what you already know, rather that staying resilient in the face of the new conceptual or people skills that your role demands removes you from the opportunity of being in a state of 'not-knowing' – where you are challenged to find new solutions. It is also the route to micromanagement, lack of delegation and can lead to the stagnation of personal and team development.

Returning to the sport analogy, you do not need to have been a technically gifted player to be a great manager or leader. Of course you need technical knowledge but you do not need to have been blessed with technical excellence. The chances of succeeding as a manager or leader in any context are limited if you are appointed only due to the prestige that has been afforded to you because of your technical ability. Better leaders have high level and high impact conceptual skills and similar people skills. If leaders do not develop their conceptual and people skills they limit their chance of creating active followership and this will ultimately place fixed boundaries around the chances of success for them and their team.

For you to be a better leader, which of these three skills would you like to develop and be better at? Which of these skills do you need to prioritise and focus on now?

Every Leader is an Emerging Leader

In some professional environments the women and men at the top of the hierarchy arc known as 'senior' leaders and those who are aspiring to get to the top of the hierarchy are known as 'emerging' leaders. The dangerous assumption here is that those at the top are no longer emerging because they have travelled and arrived. The implication is that they already have leadership sewn up and they know everything there is to know about leadership.

As you will already be aware I believe that your self is continually being constructed and reconstructed, your behaviour is always open to being altered, your esteems vary from situation to situation, your feelings and emotions are constantly moving, your brain is always changing and your needs are too. Even your own leadership skills change in response to the leadership context you are in. Everything is moving, interacting and changing: everything is emergent within you and around you. You will not be surprised that I see every leader as an emerging leader no matter where they lead or whom they lead. The term 'emerging leader' is usually applied to a leader who has begun to climb the leadership ladder within an organisation. It can also be applied to groups that begin as leaderless but allow a leader to emerge from within the group. When I use the term here I mean that the leader is emerging in terms of being ready to learn more and lead better tomorrow than they did today – that is everyone in any type of leadership role and whatever that leadership role looks like. Everyone is an emerging leader because emergence is a natural state of being.

One key strand of the inner story of the best leaders is that they lead in a way that respects and embraces emergence: their own emergence, the emergence of others and the emergence of their environment. For example, they enable new ideas, concepts, voices and perspectives to emerge. Opinions that challenge the status quo are welcomed and the people expressing them are not framed as cynical and negative. This does not mean that the leader says "yes" to every request, is all things to all people and becomes a serial compromiser, but it does mean that they create an open and honest culture. Emerging leaders are also responsive to emerging needs, difficulties and opportunities. They are open to suggestions about new practice. When they do not know or understand something they say so; they acknowledge uncertainty and the leadership benefits of not knowing.

Better leaders are not psychologically caught up in needing to be perceived as omniscient deities. They prefer people to prove them right rather than prove them wrong. If you see the world in an emergent way and value the process of emergence you will be the sort of leader who will think and respond intuitively. You will express empathy so that you can be in touch with, and respond to, what is emerging around you. Respecting emergence means being comfortable with being uncomfortable. Better leaders are comfortable with fluidity, unpredictability, vulnerability and complexity in their self, others and in their environment. When you accept that everything around you is emerging and changing you have to embrace the idea that most of your time as a leader is going to be unscripted. To truly thrive in such a leadership context you need to be able to connect with your self, with the inner story of others and with your leadership role.

Common, Distinct and Individual Needs

Being capable of meeting the needs of your team is a complex and challenging task. It is also a critical people skill. I propose that both psychologically and practically it is not possible for any leader to meet individual needs at all times. Being able to meet everyone's needs in a diverse human context can seem to be impossible; people are so different from each other that it seems like an unattainable goal. Meeting individual needs can seem overwhelming because people can be overwhelmingly individual. But it does not have to be that way.

If you have a clear model inside your mind of what people's needs are, and make that model part of your inner story, then you can work out exactly what to do to identify and to meet people's needs. I want to emphasise here that I am not referring to the standard hierarchical model that relates to our basic human survival needs such as being provided with water and food. I am referring to my personal view of human psychological needs, and my model that is not staged and hierarchical but progressively focused. I believe that these psychological needs, when met, will make every team member feel like they are important to the team and to the leader of the team. If we feel our needs are being met we commit more to whoever leads us and as a result we will perform better. To identify needs you have to ask two questions. The first and obvious question is,

"What needs do humans have?"

When I was an academic, I created and published a model of how to identify and meet psychological needs within a group or a team. My 'common, distinct, individual' model has since been published in a variety of languages. How I identify and meet needs is part of my inner story and I wrote about identifying and meeting needs because I was aware of many professional areas where 'meeting individual needs' was seen as the solution to all problems no matter how complex. This was magical thinking. Meeting individual needs is complex because people are complex. A leader, a coach or a teacher, and other people who are working with groups, cannot meet individual needs at all times. I will now describe how my needs model relates to becoming a better leader but before I do let's look at the second and less obvious question,

"Are we all the same, are some of us similar or are we all different?"

The answer to that question is "yes".
Confused? No worries, please read on.

I propose that as humans our psychological needs belong to three categories,

Common Needs
Distinct Needs
Individual Needs

The cover of this book will help you visualise what I mean and get the picture. On the outer circle are common needs, on the inner circle are distinct needs and individual needs are in the middle of the centre circle. I believe that to understand needs in a group, or a team, you always begin by focusing on what people have in common. I would also argue that focusing on what people have in common is the best way to understand people in societies, cultures and in the global community too.

In any group or team you begin by identifying *common* needs. You then focus in and begin to identify *distinct* needs. Through this progressive focusing method, almost like using a manual focus on a camera lens, you are able to see the individual clearly and identify and meet *individual* needs.

What are common needs?

Common needs are the basic psychological needs that I believe every human has in common. These include being respected, being valued as a person, being afforded dignity, feeling a sense of worth, being given a voice rather than having your voice silenced and feeling a sense of belonging. When a leader meets common needs a person in the team is in a much better position to relax and to perform well. Every person in the team should have their common needs met through the behaviour of the leader and through the behaviour of their colleagues. When meeting common needs you have to think about everyone in the team as being the same. But need identification cannot stop there.

What are distinct needs?

These are the needs that emerge from the groups or groupings that people belong to or they identify with. These include gender, race, disability, sexuality, ethnicity, culture and faith community. Distinct needs may be highly relevant to the order in which someone constructs and prioritises her or his identity. They may be critical in a person accepting who they are and being proud of who they are. Distinct needs also highlight the wonderful diversity that can exist within any group. You began to understand needs by acknowledging that everyone in the team is the same. When meeting distinct needs you have to think about groups of people as being similar.

Your identification of needs cannot stop there. You have to understand the individuality of each person or stereotyping can occur. Stereotyping happens when your mind takes a cognitive and emotional short cut to help you to categorise your world and make it more predictable. There are millions of people who prefer to live in a world that is predictable. Stereotyping creates oversimplified and incomplete perceptions about the nature and identities of individuals and groups. This becomes divisive and dangerous when the stereotypes remain unchallenged. So, let's complete the picture by moving inwards to identify individuality.

What are individual needs?

Individual needs are the needs of a particular person at a particular time in a particular context. An individual need, by definition, is a need that nobody else in the team has at that moment. The need has to be specific to one person and one person only because if more than one person in the team has the same need then that is not an individual need, it becomes a distinct or a common need. When meeting individual needs you have to think about everyone in the team as being different. You have to be conscious of what it is that makes someone unique.

Let me provide an example. I was working with a team when one of the people in the team encountered a family bereavement. No other person in the team was in that situation at that time. Coping with the loss of a loved one became an individual need within this particular team. I was able to respond immediately to that need and offer support to the person, and to the team, for as long as it was required. If there had been another person in the team dealing with bereavement then I would have had to look carefully at each situation to identify the individual need of each person who was bereaved. This would enable me to differentiate my response accordingly. We cannot assume that all individuals respond to the trauma and piercing pain of bereavement in exactly the same way.

I deliberately choose bereavement as an example because that is an individual need that can be overlooked due to the emotional discomfort of not knowing what to say or do when someone experiences a bereavement and returns to work. I also choose it to emphasise that, no matter how challenging it might be to meet an individual need, if one emerges within a team it has to be acknowledged and met.

It can be a valuable exercise to think of a member of your team and to work through my needs model to see what needs you are meeting and what needs you are not meeting. I have worked with some leaders who have done exactly that and have been surprised that they are not meeting some of the common needs of a team member, were unaware of some of the person's distinct needs and were able to identify a time when there was an individual need that was not met. One leader that I have worked with for many years has a drawing of my needs model displayed on her office wall. She told me that from time to time she randomly selects a team member and carries out a needs audit to check if their needs are being met.

Respecting diversity

You can often gain an insight into how a leader understands needs by the way they respond to questions about diversity within their team. Here is one type of reaction to responding to questions about diversity. You may have heard similar words in your workplace.

> "I treat everyone the same. I don't notice things like race or gender or disability because I only see people. They are all people to me."

Now that you have a needs model in your mind you will see that this leader will always remain in the outer circle of common needs because they are all people to him. He cannot meet distinct or individual needs because his need identification process will naturally stop at commonality. What is also concerning is that he thinks that it is a good thing to group everyone as 'people' and treat everyone the same. This prevents him from going beyond common needs because equal treatment does not create equal opportunity. Treating everyone in the team as if they are all the same cloaks individuality and prevents you from respecting the breadth of diversity, difference, disposition and orientation.

At times a leader will aim to meet common needs within a group, at other times her focus will be on distinct needs and on a different occasion she will be paying full attention to an individual need. You cannot meet the individual needs of each person all of the time. Meeting needs in a fluid way is necessary if you want to be a better leader but you have to be clear about which needs you are meeting at which times and why. Before you move on to think about your empathy skills as a leader let's allow your mind to consolidate what you have just been thinking about.

Common Needs – everyone is the same
Distinct Needs – groups of people are similar
Individual Needs – everyone is different

Empathy

Better leaders understand the lived experience of their teams and remain genuinely curious about the inner story of others. Being genuinely curious and intellectually curious keeps you open to new learning; it opens your mind. To understand lived experience you have to understand the other person's way of seeing the world and accept that it can be different to your way of seeing the world. You also need to connect with the way that others are thinking and feeling and accept that they can be feeling or thinking differently to you. You will recognise that what I am describing here is empathy.

Empathy is the ability to respond emotionally and connect with the inner story of others. There are many ways that empathy can help you to become a better leader.

Empathy and inequality

Empathy has many leadership benefits. Once you connect with the inner story of others you can understand the world from their perspective and take suitable action. For example, you can become more active in advocating for those who are being marginalised as well as create interventions that drive people to new levels of performance. Empathy can help you to challenge prejudice, inequality and discrimination. It can help you to challenge gender stereotypes such as the notion that when men express their emotions openly it is an indicator of leadership strength but when woman do the same it indicates leadership vulnerability. Understanding the world from the perspective of others can also raise awareness of gender bias such as in the existence of the 'glass ceiling': the invisible permafrost layer that prevents women from gaining the senior positions that they deserve.

For some women the glass ceiling is not a major issue because they have been able to progress within systems and receive the support of men as well as women who are already in senior positions. In some organisational structures women reach a certain point where they are prevented from moving upwards or sideways. I am acutely aware that I am only mentioning one type of bias here and that I could be mentioning many conscious or unconscious biases that are equally as important.

Empathy enables you to open your eyes to many issues of workplace inequality in all forms, allowing you to champion the behaviours and the systems that will challenge and eliminate inequality. Empathy can also ensure that you are able to make decisions that are not based on self-protection, self-justification or self-interest.

If expressing empathy can help you to become a better leader, where do you begin? What needs to happen in your mind so that you can be better at developing empathy? Now it is time to introduce you to epoché.

The stepping-stone to empathy

To develop and demonstrate empathy you must be able to suspend your judgment about others. You have to do this whether you like or dislike them as people and whether they support or undermine you as a leader. This requires a certain type of psychological flexibility that is known as epoché. Epoché is the stepping-stone to empathy. If epoché is missing as a strand of your inner story, then really understanding what it is like to see someone else's world from the point of view of standing in their shoes becomes impossible - and that's before you even think about what it must be like standing inside their mind.

Suspending your judgment about others so that you can connect with them can be a very difficult thing to do. Think about it as needing to behave like a researcher. When you engage in research you begin by getting inside your own mind so that you can identify your biases, prejudices, reservations and unexamined beliefs and set them aside. You spend time unpacking or deactivating the taken-for-granted assumptions that you make about why people are the way they are or why they behave the way they do. You are then in a better position to be able to take people and their experiences as they are presented to you, as their lived worldview, rather than how you process them to be from your lived worldview.

This is not an easy process to engage in and for some people it challenges them to break habits of thinking and being that have existed in their mind for years. But this is what has to be done so that you can remain as neutral as possible about what is being presented to you. Suspending your judgment involves accepting people as they appear to be rather than how you judge them to be.

You listen to what they tell you as their description of their world without adding your own meaning to it. To develop epoché you have to pay full attention when listening and this involves listening to what is being said as well as to what is not being said. You move beyond first impressions and resist the temptation to jump to immediate conclusions. Epoché creates empathy.

Empathy is seen as a characteristic of a 'coaching' style of leadership and coaching is the next aspect of leadership that I would like to explore. Some leaders are expected to adopt a coaching style so that they can be better at leading. Other leaders employ coaches to help develop their teams. In either situation the leader will have a concept in their mind of what coaching is and how it is different or similar to leadership.

Coaches Wear the Small Shoes

Coaching is explorative. It is another way of empowering someone to access their mind and change their inner story so that they can perform and achieve beyond their perceived capabilities in their personal or professional life. There is no finishing line to being a better you: new possibilities are always available to you and coaching can help you to achieve them. One caricature of the difference between coaching and leadership is that leaders tell you what to do and coaches ask you what you think you should do: leaders are directive and coaches are non-directive. Another is that leaders show you what to do but coaches help you learn how to do it. Coaching and leadership are different but they are also similar. If coaching and leadership were musical notes they would be part of the same harmonious chord.

Now I would like you to think back to when you were a young child please. I ask you to do this because you may have learned one of the best lessons that a coach can learn as long ago as when you were a toddler. Did your parents ever ask you to face them, reach up and hold their hands and stand on their shoes? If they did it is likely that they will have then walked around the room with you while you stood on their shoes and moved in unison with them. You may recall them doing this but dancing around the room?

Whether they were dancing or walking the process was the same: you followed their lead with your feet in your small shoes standing on top of their feet in their big shoes. This childhood experience is a meaningful metaphor for coaching because coaching is about leading and following. If a coach is driven by her or his own needs, or is on her or his own status-driven ego trip, they will want to wear the larger shoes and lead all of the time. This is the wrong way round. High impact coaching occurs when the coach is willing to wear the smaller shoes most of the time. To do so requires the coach to have complete confidence in her or his own inner story both as a coach and as a person. Yes, there will be times when a coach has to wear the big shoes. These times will include when their professional expertise and knowledge has to be shared through their openness, their stories and their insights. Coaches also have a responsibility to be educators and elevators: to guide and move people beyond their current knowledge base and to lift them up emotionally when necessary.

Coaches must also offer emotional and cognitive scaffolding to the person they are coaching to help them navigate their thoughts and emotions and change their behaviour to improve their performance. Even so, they should spend most of the time in the small shoes allowing solutions to emerge as the person being coached leads the agenda and directs the focus. It is their needs that are the priority, not the needs of the coach. If you are a coach, or a leader who adopts a coaching style, I would like to raise one key point about the psychology of coaching. When someone presents you with a problem or a challenge it will fit within a hierarchy of significance within your mind. That is perfectly natural; one way that we make meaning out of our world is by establishing what matters more to us and what matters less. Your judgment about the nature and intensity of their problem or challenge will be based upon your view of the world – every one of us is susceptible to myside bias: seeing the world of others only from where we are standing.

However, every coach must flatten their own hierarchy of significance before they begin the coaching process because it is the significance of the issue in the world of the person they are coaching that matters. That is how coaching can begin to change the world of the person who is being coached. Coaching embeds learning and enables change. We can only really understand what makes people tick by seeing the world from their perspective, not ours.

Better Leaders Give Better Praise

It is generally accepted that praise matters in an adult-child relationship but we can forget that praise matters in an adult-adult relationship too. The practice of praising other adults can disappear from some leadership radars. If this happens it is unfortunate because praise is a performance lever within a team and it can increase engagement with, and commitment to, the team. To be clear, when I refer to praise I mean praise that has the intention to encourage rather than to exploit. I also mean the type of praise that is intended to show genuine gratitude rather than exert calculated control. Praise must be about motivation rather than manipulation.

I shall now suggest five successful ways to praise that are successful in a variety of contexts. I believe they can enable better leadership.

Praise regularly

Be a praise-giver and give praise regularly. Praise should not be difficult to gain. You may know people who are proud that they do not give regular praise. People like this often feel that if they withhold praise, when they do praise a team member the praise is going to be more powerful. Unfortunately, waiting to be praised by such a leader has a demoralising impact on everybody who is lined up in the ever-increasing anticipatory queue. It is important to give praise and to give praise regularly.

Be sincere

Recently a middle manager said to me, "My boss praises me occasionally but you never believe that he means it. It is like he has suddenly remembered to do it. You always worry that there's a hidden agenda going on". Insincere praise devalues the currency of praise because people see straight through it. When you praise someone they can tell whether you are being authentic and if you believe what you are saying. Sincere praise is important because it increases the engagement of a team member to the whole team and boosts a person's sense of self. Sincerity matters.

Be timely

One method of reinforcing a desired behaviour is to seize the moment and praise the behaviour as soon you see it happening. Another is to ensure that the praise for the behaviour is timely to prevent praise from being perceived as an afterthought. In being timely we also have to take into account the personality, disposition and emotional context of the person that we are praising. There are those who like to be praised immediately. They may be indifferent about who hears the praise or they may actively enjoy the fact that others are within hearing distance. There are also those who prefer to be invited into an office, or taken aside to a quiet space and spoken to privately and in a more discreet manner. There may also be cultural issues to consider about giving praise publicly or privately. Timely praise works well when it respects individual difference and individual preference.

Be precise

Praise should always be precise. If you are precise about what you are praising you amplify the chance of reinforcing behaviour. For example, a parent of a young child might say, "well done, you have eaten nicely". Many parents of young children will recognise that phrase. 'Eating nicely' is the behaviour that is being reinforced. But this is not a precise description of behaviour, it is vague. They could use more precise praise by identifying exactly what eating nicely means – this can include the actions involved in eating nicely as well as the effort that a child has put in to eating nicely. Precise praise works for adults too. The next time that you praise someone for their presentation, or for the part that they played in delivering or winning a pitch, think about the difference between these types of statements,

"Well done, great job."
"Well done, you got your message across clearly."
"Well done. You prepared and presented well and made it very clear to the client that we could solve their problem."

You will notice that the more precise the praise the greater impact it will have.

Uncontaminated by negative criticism

Unfortunately, some people use praise as a precursor to criticism as they believe that praise softens criticism. This is like me claiming that if I tickle you under the chin with my left hand it is going to be less painful when I follow up by punching you in the groin with my right hand. The language of praise in this context usually goes something like this,

"Well done. I like it *but*..."

"I like it" is the tickle. The "but" prepares you for the body blow. Praise that is followed by criticism will be processed as criticism. The praise will go missing in the process of patterning because the word 'but' invalidates the praise at the start of the sentence. Praise hasn't softened the criticism at all; it has actually helped to harden it. If you want to praise someone and follow the praise with constructive feedback, the language used is very important. Instead of saying "I like it but..." say "I like it *and* ..." This allows you to complete the sentence with a question that encourages the person to think about improvements, "I like it (pause) and have you thought about..."

Talking of questions...

Better Leaders Ask Better Questions

There are many different types of questions available to us. Questioning allows your mind to imagine and pretend what the familiar might be like if it was unfamiliar, to disrupt and agitate your normal patterns of thinking, to take risks and to project what might be possible in the future. Questioning is a process that enables you to alter the content of your mind. You will have noticed that I have asked you many questions as you have read this book. I have not asked you questions like,

Is a swimming pool still a swimming pool if it has no water in it?

Does birdsong exist without a bird?

What does the colour red look like from behind?

I have asked reflective questions. These are questions that invite you inside your mind to engage in consciously thinking about your inner story. Better leaders know that questioning and reflection helps to change your world because reflection is a process that can change your focus, your emotions and your actions. Reflection is an emotional as well as a cognitive process. Reflection does not have to be a solitary activity and nor does it have to be a long drawn-out process either; it can be collaborative, intuitive and instant. Sometimes it can be beneficial not to over-think. Questions help you find solutions and the quality of the questions that you ask will influence the nature of solutions that emerge.

Better leaders ask leading questions

It has become a cliché for leaders to say, "What we face here is not a problem it is a challenge". Whether it is a leadership cliché or not, to a degree, this makes sense.

You may well have heard people describe a challenge as a 'problem'. Inside the mind there is an issue here because the name or the label that we give to something will always influence how we think about it and respond to it. The "is this a problem or is this a challenge?" question is a leading question because it leads you into considering the language that you use and the orientation that you have adopted towards a task: am I encountering a problem or am I facing a challenge? It is not only leaders that help you to shape your reality; the language that you use does so too. You rise to a challenge. You do not rise to a problem.

Another difficulty with the concept of something being a 'problem' is that it is possible to talk about a problem for hours yet at the end of the conversation all you have is more information about the problem. This is why people who focus on their problems feel worse when they talk at length about them. Unless you spend time talking about exceptions to the problem, a problem will keep you trapped on a mental treadmill. It is more helpful to think in terms of challenges because in your mind you immediately move from a problem framework into a challenge framework. It allows you to change your perspective on what is happening.

Consider what your current challenge is. Maybe you find it difficult to have professional conversations that might result in confrontation? Maybe you have a relationship with your boss that is based on trust and respect – this is normally positive but in your case she does not respect you and you do not trust her. It might be that you cannot work out how to get from excellent to exceptional in a sporting context? Whatever your challenge might be, you will make quicker progress towards finding a solution by thinking of it as a challenge rather than a problem. This is because problems create problem-focused thinking whereas challenges create solution-focused thinking. If you do have a challenge and you are looking for a solution then we must return to the value of reflecting and asking questions. In this case you need to ask solution-focused or solution-oriented questions. Here are three questions that can help,

"What do I need to stop doing?"
"What do I need to start doing?"
"What should I continue doing because it is working well?"

These are good examples of leading questions that begin to move you towards solutions. I have worked with teams who use these questions in order to generate solutions and create higher levels of team performance. But there are even better questions: questions that will help you to find higher quality and quicker solutions. They are the beautiful questions. You just need to know what they are.

Better Leaders Ask Beautiful Questions

I would like to focus on two beautiful questions that are solution-focused gold dust. You can ask and answer them when you encounter any challenge. As a leader you can ask these questions to your whole team and to individuals so that you can help them to find fast solutions to their challenges. They are also useful questions to have in your mind for any situation where you or others feel sticky or stuck. The first is the 'miracle' question. It can also be referred to as the 'magic wand' question depending upon whom you are asking the question to and the context in which it is being asked.

The miracle question

I recommend this question if you are a parent or if you work with children. It is a great help when they find it difficult to imagine a solution to their challenges. I also use the question with adults too and so I also give it the same resounding recommendation if you work in a leadership position. Of course, I recommend it as a question that you can ask your self when you are imagining how you might change your inner story.

I structure the question like this,

> "When you go to bed tonight, imagine that while you sleep and dream a miracle takes place. When you wake up in the morning everything is exactly as you want it to be. Please tell me what is happening."

If you were to ask a young child this question you replace "a miracle takes place" with "someone waves a magic wand". This is such a beautiful question because when the person answering the question describes what is happening after they have woken up it gives them permission to imagine their best hopes. Be honest, how often do you give people permission to imagine their best hopes? How often do you allow your self to imagine your best hopes? Once they have identified their best hopes they will have started to map out what some of the key solutions would look like for them. You can ask them to prioritise their solutions and begin to establish how they might make each one happen. What I also like about this question is that it encourages your mind to instantly think about what things would be like if they were different. It will change your mind in a second.

Please try it. It really does work.

One cautionary note here: if you are answering the question for your self, ensure that you keep the answer optimistic but also realistic. If you are asking others you will notice that some people will answer the question by describing a world where the solutions they hope for may be impossible to achieve. This provides an opportunity for you to help them to ground their answers in reality and to look at their challenge more realistically.

The question from the cluttered shop

There is a personal context for my second beautiful question. My mum was a one-woman riot and my dad loved to make people laugh. My parents came to the UK from Ireland to provide better life opportunities for their children than the ones they had. I grew up in a culturally diverse working-class immigrant community in the midlands. I still feel an intense sense of disappointment when I hear politicians and social commentators say that the key to social cohesion in diverse communities is integration and tolerance. I wonder if the people making these statements have ever lived in a community like the one where I enjoyed my childhood? If they had, they would understand that integration and tolerance are never going to be fundamental to cohesion in any community – inclusion and acceptance are.

My dad adapted from working on the docks in Ireland to working night shifts in a tool-making factory in England. He worked with a group of Irish men who were held together by camaraderie and mischief. All of the men had been geographically relocated but some of the men had become psychologically dislocated; melancholic laments about their forty-shades-of-green homeland offering emotional comfort and social bonding when the weekend beer began to flow. Economically times became tough and the factory closed down. My dad struggled to find another job and became a self-employed window cleaner – or "vision technician" as he liked to call it when he met people who he thought were being grandiose. My mum worked part-time as a Silver Service waitress. She quickly learned how to serve food from a platter to a plate by manipulating a serving fork and spoon with the fine and gross motor skills of a surgeon. Eventually she found a new job too, working in a role where she offered support to people with disabilities. My mum and dad were never given the title 'leader' but, like many immigrants, they had inner stories that illuminate what leadership means. Leadership exists in many forms.

A regular event from my childhood provides the context for the second beautiful question. You would probably expect a psychologist to assert the value of an uncluttered mind but, instead, I would like to open the door and invite you inside a cluttered shop.

My friend Mustak lived with his parents above their family business. With products and produce piled high on the pavement, precariously frozen in a state of collapse, their family business stood out amongst an eclectic parade of shops that served local community needs. These shops included a butcher, a barber and the shop that every community seemed to have in those days where you could get your shoes repaired 'while-u-wait' and take advantage of the waiting time by having new keys cut for your house and getting a trophy engraved if you felt so inclined.

Sometimes I would sit with Mustak on randomly strewn, newly delivered, saffron-stained sacks. We would observe his father. Even at a young age, I would watch with curiosity and intrigue. I was fascinated by how Mustak's dad greeted his customers as they entered the cluttered shop. He seemed to know everybody's first name. Inside his head he stored nuggets of knowledge about each customer that enabled him to individualise the content of his conversations. He even individualised his rapport. He could be flamboyant, formal, jocular, serene. He made customers feel as if they were long-lost members of his family being welcomed warmly back into his home. I was also enchanted by the way he said goodbye to his customers. I noticed that, as each person left his shop, Mustak's dad would say exactly the same thing, every time, no matter who the person was or what faith community or culture the person belonged to,

"You will come back soon, In Shaa Allah."

If you look carefully you will see that his benevolent spiritual blessing was preceded by an expectation and a command that became comfortably embedded in the unconscious mind of his customers. Mustak's dad's inner story must have been not only about being open and respectful but also about being the sort of person who was a social and commercial magician.

The final question I would like to offer to you is a question that I learnt from Mustak's dad and have used many times in my professional career. I may need to remind you, or inform you, that in those days in small shops the customer would state what they wanted to buy and the shop owner would get the product for them. The customer would provide the first line of the script as they approached Mustak's dad with a request. With a genial smile he would always reply in the same manner. The scene went something like this:

"Can I have some bread please?"

"And?"

"We are running out of milk at home, so can I have some milk please?"

"And?"

"Well, I guess I could buy some soap while I am here. We always need soap."

"And?"

"Erm...let me think...I may as well get a newspaper and find out what is happening in the world."

"And?"

And so it continued. Clearly the question was part of his sales technique, but what a beautiful question it is. "And" posed as a question, is a single word that opens your mind to infinite possibilities. In your mind it transforms to,

"And what else?"

This immediately encourages your brain to pattern for new options and to search for new solutions.

When you feel stuck and feel that you cannot find a solution to a leadership challenge or a personal challenge you can always try sleeping on it and letting your unconscious work on it. Due to the way that your unconscious mind associates, inoculates and consolidates it may have found a solution for you before you wake up.

If not, when you wake up, you can ask your self the question from the cluttered shop. If that does not work you can always take a more conscious route and imagine that, while you were asleep, someone waved a magic wand or a miracle happened.

The Short Story

You can lead from the front, you can lead from the centre or you can do both – but leading from the back can be problematic.

Leadership skills move up and down.

We all have common, distinct and individual needs.

Epoché is the stepping-stone to empathy.

Equality of opportunity does not mean equal treatment.

Leadership is an expression of your inner story.

People like to be included and accepted not integrated and tolerated.

Praise works best when it is regular, sincere, timely, precise and uncontaminated by negative criticism.

Coaches wear the smaller shoes.

Better leaders ask the beautiful questions.

Chapter Ten
Being A Higher Performing Team

A team is a community of mind and therefore every team writes and lives its inner story. There is something special about being in a higher performing team and there is also something special happening in a higher performing team. Being in the team and contributing to what is happening in the team creates a special togetherness that can result in memories, relationships and the type of friendships that last a lifetime.

This chapter specifically applies to teams and to the essence of higher performance in teams. Throughout the chapter I refer to 'higher performing teams' rather than to 'high performing teams' as performance, like love, should not have limits. You can always aim for higher performance; every team can strive to perform better. This chapter also links with other chapters. If you are reading the chapters in order of their importance in your world, you may not have read the section on common, distinct and individual needs in chapter nine. This section is especially relevant to higher performance because a higher performing team is a team where the needs of the whole team, of groups and of individuals are identified, understood and met. Meeting needs is exceptionally important because members of higher performing teams are not just performers; first and foremost they are people.

In chapter four I described how behaviour can bounce and this knowledge is relevant to enabling higher performance too. In chapter six I outlined the inner story for being more successful. Most of the content of that chapter applies to teams as well as individuals, including never fearing failure, focusing more on the process than the outcome, loving to win more than hating to lose, focusing on the right thing and accepting that if you want to arrive you have to travel.

I have worked with consistently higher performing teams and I have also worked in consistently higher performing teams.

There is something deeper that occurs within these teams that psychologically aligns every individual and creates the togetherness that transforms performance and allows the team's talent to be expressed fully and freely. That 'something deeper' is the inner story of the team. Knowing the inner story of the team enables you to become the sort of team who constantly strives for, and achieves, higher performance.

Every team is constantly shaping and constructing its emerging reality. Like individuals, the team has to know what its inner story is and whether it is working for them. Knowing your inner story is the fast way to improving team participation and performance but a similar challenge arises here as it does for individuals – there are teams who do not know what their inner story is. The team inner story needs to be known rather than unknown so that the team can take control of it and transform both the process and outcomes of performance. Just because everyone is in the team we cannot assume that everyone knows what the team is.

In this chapter, amongst other things, you will hear from a media business that changed its inner story and transformed its performance. I shall explain why I believe there is an 'I' in 'team' and will highlight the psychological dangers of confusing a higher performing team with a family. It is now taken-for-granted knowledge that characteristics of higher performing teams include having clear performance goals and containing people with complementary skills. If you are in a team and hear someone say, "nobody told me there was a communication problem here" this is a definite indicator that you are not in a higher performing team. Effective and efficient communication is another characteristic of higher performing teams. I will not be covering any of these areas here as they are very well covered elsewhere. I am far more interested in what is at the soul of every higher performing team, what it is that creates freely expressed performance, what it is that ensures that the whole team is together, sticks together and stays together, what it is that develops a mindset defined and driven by shared meaning and purpose, what it is that helps everyone to serve the team – and all of that stems from the inner story of the team.

I will explain how you can find your team inner story, how I have found team inner stories and why finding the inner story matters. My commitment to confidentiality prevents me from providing details of the specifics of my work, always carried out behind the scenes, with the teams that I have worked with. However, at this point I can provide you with an overview from a business that used inner story work to understand their shared reality, to increase their shared belief, change their culture and raise their game.

The Hat Trick Story

The following example from Hat Trick Productions provides an insight into how discovering, knowing and changing your inner story can transform performance. Hat Trick is one of the UK's truly independent television production companies. It is particularly well known for the long-running and iconic UK series *Have I Got News For You*. Hat Trick is a multi award-winning creator and producer of internationally successful television programmes in the comedy, entertainment and drama genres.

This brief insight is offered from the perspective of Jimmy Mulville, the owner and managing director. Jimmy kindly offered to provide a description of how Hat Trick changed its inner story because he has already spoken in public about my work with his business. These are Jimmy's words:

"There's no question that when I called Tim I was having a bad day. My company was saddled with a huge debt having been partly acquired by a private equity business. My co-founder had left, the company's commercial director had left and we hadn't sold a new television show for some time. I was stressed and at a loss. I phoned Tim, whom I already knew, and I explained what was happening at my company and how I felt about it.

I told him about the difficult situation we were in and said that I didn't have a clear idea of what to do next. I felt stuck. I felt frightened. His reply was typically clear and incisive,

"You sound like you are having a crisis?"

"Yes, you can definitely say that."

"Good," he replied, "Never waste a crisis!"

And so a period of soul-searching began.

We started by finding what Tim referred to as the 'inner story' of my business so that we could discover what was really going on within it rather than what we thought was going on within it. Tim has a way of digging deep and then digging deeper and the exact narrative of my business became evident. We followed this up by Tim getting inside the minds of the key individuals who were driving the business, including me. We uncovered our own inner stories and what they meant for us personally and professionally. This whole process enabled us to examine the myths that had grown within the company as well as confront the delusions under which some of us were laboring. Tim led us through this crucial task of unearthing and facing the truth. He helped us to notice, accept and admit where we were getting it wrong and to reaffirm the practices that were beneficial to us. Hat Trick embarked on the road to recovery.

We changed our narrative and created a new one. We bought the business out of its arrangement with the bank. We also changed our culture. For the first time people from across the business, some of whom I had hardly spoken to, were now having open and at times awkward conversations with me about what it was like for them to work at the company. We grew as a business and as individuals.

One person wrote to me when they were leaving the business. He said that as a result of his time at Hat Trick he was now "a better professional, a better husband and a better father." In my business we all come to work for more than just the money. For a time, and after a long period of continued success, my company had lost its way and was looking into the abyss. We needed to get our narrative back on track but we didn't know how.

It is clear to me looking back that Tim's intervention was vital in our renaissance. As a result of the work we did with him, and the work we continue to do with him, we are a healthy company built on healthy relationships. Tim asks challenging and brave questions unflinchingly and yet he manages to do so with compassion and humour. He's a one-off.

I'm so glad I called him on that day when I thought I was losing it!"

Being in the Team

Jimmy's words offer an insight into how important the inner story of a team is and also provides a context for what you will be reading about. Allow me to return to how I opened the chapter. I deliberately separated 'being' in a team from 'doing' in a team. Whilst being and doing help to form the culture of a team, my view is that the foundation of higher performance in teams is based more on the 'being' than it is on the 'doing'.

I would argue that without clarifying and changing the 'being' aspect, a team places limits around both its performance and its culture. If a team moves to performance before it has given full consideration to being, it places boundaries around achievement. Higher performance in teams is founded upon every person in the team, and everyone closely associated with the team, knowing exactly what it means to 'be' in the team.

What does it mean to 'be' in the team?

I am not referring to rules of engagement here. I am talking about the shared story, the story that is constructed and then reconstructed about what it means to *be* in a team. This is the shared story that psychologically unifies the team. Being in a team is about much more than executing the activities or tasks that the team is aiming to be successful at. It is about how each individual psychologically connects with the team and believes in the team, it relates to being mutually accountable and interdependent within the team and results in everyone knowing exactly what being in the team means. Being in the team determines how individuals within the team participate and connect with each other.

I have worked with teams who have never even considered that they have an inner story and therefore had no idea how powerful it was in influencing their current and future performance. These types of teams are assumption-driven rather than inner-story driven and once such teams work on their inner story their performance always improves. You cannot achieve consistently higher performance if you depend on each individual doing what they assume to be right for the team. There are two main challenges for the team if this situation occurs. Firstly, everyone is consciously and unconsciously operating on her or his own assumptions about what it means to be in the team. This creates the potential for worrying variations in how people interpret what commitment behaviours are required and what the team values are and mean. Secondly, individuals can alter team process disproportionately, again either actively or unconsciously, when no explicit collective process or perspective exists. This is a barrier to higher performance because it prevents the team from harnessing and exploiting the experience, expertise and potentials of the team as a team. I have also worked with teams who would like their performance to improve. They might be conscious of team dynamic issues or poor performance outcomes or they may already be successful but want to increase their level and consistency of their performance. They have a sense that something needs to change but they just cannot grasp what that something is. They may refer to it as team culture, team behaviour or place the blame on individual personalities and people – but at the heart of the issue is always what it means to be in the team. The shared meaning of the team is central to the analysis of team performance because every team creates their shared reality and everyone performs according to their reality.

I accept that, so far, talking of 'being' and 'shared reality' may sound abstract or academic or even detached from the day-to-day reality of what is happening in teams. However, I would argue that they are both fundamental to the day-to-day reality of what happens in teams. Being and doing are fundamental when a team performs, as well as when a team prepares to perform.

Therefore, to ground what I am saying, I shall now go into the practical detail of team inner story including how to find it and what a team inner story can look like. I will describe the method that I use for eliciting a team's inner story and also describe strands of team inner stories for you to reflect on. You can examine whether your team knows its inner story. You can also reflect on what your team can do to discover it and whether all of it or some of it needs changing in order to improve performance.

Know your Inner Story

Remember, a team is a community of mind. Each individual in the team will have their own reality and their own perceptions of what it means to be in the team. If this occurs certain personalities will rise to the fore while others remain in the background. This can enable those who shout the loudest to have a disproportionate impact on the inner story of the team. It also makes it possible for the most manipulative team members to work hard to take control of the team dynamic. A team cannot depend on the talent of each individual to mysteriously combine and create higher performance. Similarly, a team cannot depend on the reality of individuals to somehow magically combine as a collective mind to create the same outcome. This why teams need to gain clarity about their shared reality – it is a key driver of team performance.

Being unaware of the team inner story contributes to variance in performance and limits the potential for the team to learn and grow together. Knowing it increases the understanding of each individual about what is needed to optimise performance as well as making explicit what team members can expect from each other. This will increase commitment, collaboration and confidence within the team as well as enabling freedom of expression. It can also have the advantage of promoting distributed leadership within the team rather than single leadership of the team.

It is always possible for a leader or manager to impose an inner story upon a team so that their personal reality becomes the shared reality of the team. When this happens the lack of team ownership of their story can generate difficulties for the team. When you create a team inner story together it is a shared story, when someone imposes one upon you it is their story, not yours. It will certainly feel that way and especially so during challenging times.

The inner story of the team is also an important part of team intelligence. It influences what the team understands and knows about its task and informs how it can be delivered successfully. It directs the team in how to behave when they perform well and when they are under-performing. Over time it will provide the team with a framework for resilience and enable them to stay in the game and bounce back from adversity. It creates a performance culture and climate where there is clarity about what every team member agrees to have in common with each other. It also encourages a team to be mature enough to look beyond the team for help and support when necessary. Teams really are complex phenomena. They are also organic and dynamic: people leave and new people arrive. Inner story clarity enables new team members to be inducted and included quicker than they would be in teams who do not make the inner story explicit. By explicit I mean clearly communicated and known.

Every team member should be able to articulate a team's inner story. This is why I always recommend that a team's inner story must have no more than three strands to it so that it can be easily remembered and put into practice. Knowing does not mean having it printed on a mouse-mat near your computer or having it written on a poster in an office or even having it emblazoned across a wall. Knowing means that individuals within the team should be able to carry the team inner story around inside their mind so that it exists unconsciously as well as consciously, will influence individual and team behaviour and, whenever necessary, can be called upon to be evaluated.

How to Find the Inner Story of Your Team

I shall now describe one method that I use for finding the inner story of a team. It involves collecting, analysing and discussing evidence so that the team can have an inner story that optimises its capacity for higher performance.

Collect the evidence

A shared reality is critically important in a team. If we are teammates, I need to know that you see the team in the same way that I do and that we both understand what key concepts, such as commitment and respect, mean and look like. When discovering the inner story you have to access people's reality. You are helping the team to answer the main inner story question about what sort of team they are and what it means to be them. You can pose many questions that enable you to access people's reality and understand the interpretations they place upon their world. In terms of eliciting an inner story you may want to explore, amongst other things, specific words that people use to describe the team, what people see as the strengths of the team, their concerns about the team, how they think performance can improve, what their best hopes are for the team and how they conceptualise what the team is. When you have everyone's answers they will include a range of perceptions and interpretations, all of which are contributing to the current inner story of the team. Varying meanings, opinions, assumptions, biases and beliefs are often at the basis of the shared reality of a team that has not engaged in this process before.

Get grounded

For those who are interested in research, when I discover the inner story of a team I use a research methodology known as grounded theory to analyse the data I have gained from my discussion with each individual member of the team. When you use grounded theory you get what you find rather than get what you set out to look for. Grounded theory allows you to analyse what is emerging. Whatever emerges from the discussions or interviews with team members is what emerges. The outcomes are not predetermined. For example, a team leader might insist that the team is emotionally immature and insist that this is definitely the main cause of poor performance or team disintegration. When you look for the team inner story you do not structure your questions to prove if she or he is right or wrong. You ask open questions and find out what themes emerge. Emotional immaturity might emerge as an issue for the team but it also might not. There are usually some surprises that emerge too. Using grounded theory means that I can present the current inner story of the team back to the team, not as my opinion, or anyone else's for that matter, but as reliable data that has been gained through robust analysis. You can also take a less research-heavy route. When you do this you will find that you have lots of responses and lots of different themes that create one big team story. When you have all of these responses you can look at which are the most common and present those as the strands of the team inner story as it currently exists. You are more likely to be open to scrutiny but it is another way of gaining the inner story.

Talk about the evidence

Now that you have the current story, the team has to accept what has been presented back to them. The team will follow their acceptance of the inner story by answering a series of questions that allow them to establish if the inner story is working for them. These could include:

Is the inner story what we thought it would be?

What are the surprises and what do they mean for us?

What individual and team behaviour does this inner story promote?

To what degree should this inner story be different to enable higher performance?

Some or all of the current inner story may need changing as sometimes teams have limiting beliefs or are engaging in limiting behaviours that they are not aware of.

The next stage of the process involves the team prioritising the three key strands to their inner story: the three ways of 'being' that they believe will assist the team in achieving higher performance. The three strands become the new inner story. Once the new inner story is established it has to be accepted and agreed by all. Once agreed it becomes the new way of being within the team and defines what is expected of everyone within the team. It also defines what the team is.

Restricting Your Game

I have stated that team inner stories should have no more than three strands. So that you can begin to reflect on the strands that might work for you and for your team I will provide examples of real-world inner story strands that I have discovered. Three strands have not worked well for teams and three have. All six strands are taken from six different team contexts and every single context has been anonymised. The first three strands were restricting team performance.

Our way is the best way

This is quite a common inner story strand for businesses that have become brand arrogant or believe that the personality, profile and perception of their brand will ensure long-term market dominance. It is common amongst arrogant teams in other environments too. Doing things how you have always done them can restrict performance unless you are already world-leaders in your field. Even then, there will inevitably come a point where flexibility, adaptability and doing things differently will be required.

Arrogance can cause complacency. Complacency can cause you to stand still. When you stand still in a competitive environment there will always be others who are perceptive, persistent and determined enough to overtake you. Your way might be the best way but you have to make sure that you are always seeking a better way to keep you in your position at the top.

Intelligence matters

I meet this inner story strand from time to time in teams that place a high value on cognitive intelligence often more so than they do on emotional intelligence. The performance downside here is that when teams rate cognitive intelligence so highly they can create a culture where everyone has to air a point of view and everyone has to be heard – of course they do, they are all so intelligent that they must be heard. This promotes the type of culture where people can end up in wall-to-wall meetings, meetings about meetings and where it can take months for decisions to be made. This strand also has implications for what happens in companies who pitch for business. If you lose a pitch and you value cognitive intelligence so highly it is easy to dismiss the decision not to choose your idea as being the wrong decision. When a client decides not to go with what you were pitching it is obviously their problem. Psychologically, you *have* to see it as being their problem and nothing to do with the quality of your pitch because you need to validate your intelligence.

Otherwise you have to question the high value that you are placing on cognitive ability in the team.

What happens in these types of situations is that the team moves onto the next business pitch without analysing, in an honest and objective fashion, why their ideas did not win the pitch or why their communication was not successful. This creates and sustains a culture of denial, mediocrity and repetition of mistakes. Another performance downside here is that moving on without analysis fails to create new knowledge about what can be done better next time.

Hard work matters

Just like the other two strands, on the surface, this strand sounds vital for the inner story of a team. For many teams it is. Of course hard work matters and there is validity in having and expecting a steadfast work ethic. However, the downside here is that in teams where hard work matters it is very easy for team members to become stressed and over-stretched to the point that they feel unappreciated and downtrodden. Individual wellbeing is the first victim in these situations with team wellbeing in hot pursuit.

It is also possible that if working hard matters to the team, when times are tough the decision will be to work even harder – when working harder might not be the solution at all. It may even be counterproductive. If what you are currently doing is unsuccessful, working harder on the wrong thing is not going to be a recipe for future success; working smarter, differently and focusing on the right thing is.

Raising Your Game

Here are three inner story strands that have helped teams to improve their performance in a competitive context. They have been discussed by the whole team and agreed by the whole team. They are taken from three different contexts and are relative to the contexts that the teams operate in. The next three strands were raising team performance:

We train like we play

Whilst this may seem particularly relevant to sports teams the concept can apply to any team where preparation is critical. You cannot suddenly and consistently switch on your performance in the performance moments that matter. You have to prepare to win and that includes every individual within the team preparing in the right way. If the team is in a context where they 'train' more often than they play then full focus and commitment is required from everyone when the team trains. One performance upside of this strand is that you do not need a person in an identified leadership role to make a team member accountable for lack of full commitment as any team member will have the permission to do so. That is an outcome of everyone agreeing to be this way in the team; they have agreed to train like they play. This strand enables team leadership to be distributed, making the team more democratic.

It empowers every team member to demand that her or his colleagues are committed to the inner story of the team. This will harness the power of the team as a team. This matters because there are times when the wave can be far more powerful than the surfer. This strand also offers a fast way to address issues that relate to whole team performance as well as the performance of individuals within the team. What the team permits the team promotes.

Stand up for your expertise

This became a successful strand of an inner story for a team that was lacking in confidence as a team, but contained many confident individuals. To explain what I mean let's change the context and imagine this was a creative business and a client had asked the team to design a creative brief for a new product. The brief was returned to the client and the team had decided that the product in the brief should be yellow. Now let's imagine that the client calls back and says that they do not want yellow, initially they had not really thought about the importance of the colour but having seen the brief they now want the product to be green.

A confident business and team would stand up for what they believe to be right both creatively and commercially in such a context. They would stand up for their expertise and would respond to the client by explaining why the product should be yellow. Of course, the client may be right so the team would never dismiss green outright, but the reason for selecting yellow would be comprehensively communicated to the client and discussed further. Instead, in this business, if the client suddenly wanted green they got green. Certain team members would work into the early hours to ensure that the client had the green product by the opening of business the following day. Obviously I am simplifying the context and anonymising the business but the concept and the principle is clear.

When the team introduced this new strand to their inner story and stood up for their own expertise they were more confident and more assertive with clients and both parties gained benefit as a consequence. Green may have turned out to be the best decision but that conclusion would be arrived at by a process of confident collaborative evaluation rather than by one party cowering into a dark apologetic corner.

Also, the team was further restricted because of a culture where many people were expressing their views on the expertise of others. I am not talking about the sharing of ideas across disciplines or perspectives I am referring to illusory expertise that is expressed as knowledge, dressed as wisdom and offered freely and regularly. If this team were a football team, it would be similar to the team psychologist expressing a view on how the medical team is rehabilitating a player who has a ruptured anterior cruciate ligament and believing that view to be absolutely valid.

What I am describing may sound like madness but everyone having a view on everything can be enabled and become routine in any team where the inner story is not clear. It does happen and that is not all that can happen. Inner story lack of clarity can also cause free-floating anxiety and paranoia for those who have a private self that is anxious about their capacity to perform well in their role within a team. Their internal anxiety is projected outwards so that their outer facing self engages in behaviours that are based upon role justification. The need to be seen as having expertise beyond your own designated area, even if it is illusory expertise, is one of many forms of role justification and self-justification. It had gone so far for this particular team that a free-for-all feedback jamboree had developed with the obvious implications for team culture and performance. With a new inner story the freedom to give and receive feedback remained but now there were new and clearly communicated boundaries. It was agreed by everyone in the team that feedback was only appropriate when it had clear performance value and where the expertise of others overlapped or was connected with your own. Loosely connected was fine as long as the connection was evident and mutually agreed.

My success is your success

This strand comes from a context where a whole team can succeed but there are times when team success can look as if it is due to the actions of one individual. For some teams where the performance of an individual can be highlighted or amplified this can cause an undercurrent of envy or resentment within the team, especially if the same person seems to be the one who takes the plaudits and adulation for the team's performance and outcomes. My view is that higher performing teams can be emotionally sensitive teams. From an external perspective confidence may appear to be rock-solid, however it can become vulnerable and fragile and therefore cannot be left unattended. If the inner story of the team includes 'my success is your success' everyone is committed to the success of everybody else and emotional generosity becomes the accepted norm. This reinforces whole team confidence. Also, if an individual does perform in a way that has clearly helped the team to win, they ensure that they acknowledge the contribution of the team. Thus the team is validated, can enjoy celebrating an individual member's success and team togetherness is deepened.

Have you ever paid full attention to how a sports team celebrates when a member of the team scores? Although this may appear to be a spontaneous reaction, in some teams it may well have been agreed beforehand that when someone scores everyone will celebrate in some way. The action of celebrating together provides a very clear manifestation of togetherness within the team and can also be an additional psychological blow to the opposition players who have to stand by and observe the celebration.

Nobody in a team, no matter how exceptional they are, can win on their own.

Added Benefits

I will use the context of sports teams to illuminate more benefits of knowing your inner story and to answer some key questions that are relevant to team composition and performance behaviour. You will be able to transfer them to your own team context.

Who should be in the team?

When you know your inner story it can inform team recruitment and selection as you need to have people in the team who live the inner story of the team and believe in the inner story of the team. In some sports teams the inner story might also be the platform for selecting the team captain. To those outside of the team the selection of a particular player as captain may be a surprise or even a shock. For example, outside of the team people may expect a captain to be loud, dominant and demonstrative but the inner story of the team may not require that type of personality at all. It might require someone who the whole team respects because they embody the inner story of the team both on and off the pitch and because they demand that everyone else in the team does the same. This principle applies to leaders of business teams: the way that they live the inner story of the team demonstrates authentic leadership.

The maturity of the team

Knowing the inner story of the team speeds up the process of team maturity because everyone knows exactly what it means to be in the team and works on it every day. This prevents the development of cliques and collusive coalitions that can occur in teams. It also reduces the negative aspects of conflict. Inner story awareness provides a context for respectfully addressing issues relating to team performance or individual performance within the team. It also enables the team to deal with emerging tensions before they become problematic and destructive. This adds new dimensions to the team dynamic and to team wellbeing.

Staying grounded

Knowing the inner story grounds team members. It enables them to remain committed, patient and to believe in what the team is doing collectively whilst always knowing that should the inner story prove not to be working they have the power to adapt and change it. One benefit here is that a team who knows their inner story is a team that will not require micromanagement. Team members can be afforded suitable and respectful levels of autonomy. Knowing your inner story also grounds solidarity within the team. The formula for higher performance works like this: I know what I can expect and accept from you, you know what you can expect and accept from me and we all know what we can expect and accept from each other. We hold each other to account to this when necessary, creating individual accountability as well as mutual accountability. Clarity about the team's inner story also keeps a focus on actions that can be taken in the here and now: what can I or we do today that will help team performance to improve?

A story you can share

When you know your inner story it is a story that can be shared outside of the team. Sometimes people can figure it out through their interactions with you. They pick up messages about your team identity or your brand. There are times when it can be helpful to openly communicate it to others. In doing so you make a statement about what the team is as well as what the inner story of the team is: this is what we are, this is what we stand for, this is what we do and this is why we do it. There are other occasions when you may also have to openly communicate the inner story. For example, if those outside of the team bring the resilience or the creativity of the team into question, their negativity or desire to shape your reality for you may need to be challenged. You do this by reinforcing that inside the team you know that you have an abundance of, and belief in, the qualities that they are questioning.

Trust, Respect and Togetherness

Two things are critical in terms of creating togetherness within a team: first of all trust and first of all respect. That is how deeply intertwined they are. I am unable to prioritise them. Trust and respect are the constructs on which team togetherness is built.

Everyone in the team has to be trusted to demonstrate the commitment behaviours that enable the team to perform at its best. They also have to be trusted to live the inner story of the team and model the behaviours and values that are required. In a higher performing team the espoused values are the lived values; in teams where performance is poor or inconsistent there can be a gulf between espoused values and lived values. Everyone also has to be respected for what they offer to the team both as a professional and as a person. Trust and respect are the lifeblood of team togetherness.

When you are trusted and respected in a team you feel a sense of belonging and you are ready to give everything to the team, make sacrifices for the team and serve the team. Explicit trust and respect removes anxiety and replaces it with belief. It prevents opportunities for team members to exploit, blame or manipulate each other and increases the emotional wellbeing of the team. Trust and respect within a team enables team members to develop their relationships. Trust and respect are the pillars of performance cohesion.

Do we have to like each other?

The issue of whether people in teams should like each other often arises when I work with teams on their inner story. It creates a powerful dynamic if team members do like each other. 'Trust', 'respect' and 'like' are also a perfect triangular combination for creating social cohesion. Although it might be desirable for people in a team to like each other it is not critical that everyone within a team likes each other. What is critical is that everyone in the team trusts and respects each other. Performance cohesion and performance togetherness have to come before social cohesion and social togetherness in any competitive context. There are examples where individuals within higher performing teams have not liked each other as people but team performance and team togetherness remained high because they trusted and respected each other as professionals. Part of the inner story of higher performing teams is that they evaluate and enjoy the relationships and the sense of togetherness that they have. They understand how it helps a sense of 'self' and a sense of 'team' to grow. Togetherness is critical.

It is always possible for a team that is high on togetherness but low on talent to beat a team that is high on talent but low on togetherness.

A Higher Performing Team is Not a Family

There are occasions when people's minds confuse being in a higher performing team with being in a family. This is because, on occasions, that is exactly how it can feel. I have already stated that a higher performing team generates a strong sense of belonging. This feeling can be amplified when the team is composed of people from a range of cultures and backgrounds where diversity is accepted and embraced. What could potentially be a collection of culturally diverse individuals now becomes a team where trust and respect abound. This really can feel like belonging to a family, every individual is accepted with unconditional positive regard. I know of businesses that welcome new employees with a letter that openly states "welcome to our family" as a way of aiming to emphasise togetherness within the business and I have also encountered "we are a family" as a strand of an inner story on occasions in teams. So why am I so concerned?

Being in some families is a wonderful place to be. You feel valued, heard and loved; you are allowed to be who you are and who you want to be in an environment of unconditional positive regard. However, the family model is not the best model for a higher performing team. This is mainly due to some of the dynamics that can occur within a family model. Let's be honest, some families are emotionally volatile and they enable and validate destructive and passive-aggressive behaviour. You might argue that some teams can be like this too but there are even more issues within the family model that are problematic for teams and their performance.

Openness and honesty are essential in higher performing teams. In some family units there are family members who are not open and honest with each other. In some families people keep secrets and they talk about each other behind backs rather than having face-to-face conversations. Lack of honesty is a performance restrictor in teams; giving honest feedback and being open to receiving honest feedback is a performance enabler. I have led meetings with teams where the level of honesty would be a surprise to those who are not used to these types of environments. As well as supporting each other people are also honest about what they need from each other and this is one of the ways that they demand excellence. What I am referring to here is definitely not sugarcoated honesty but it is given in a sensitive and respectful manner to ensure that nobody feels publicly humiliated. The aim of being honest is to improve the performance of the team and not to air personal gripes or grievances to humiliate others. Being honest with others and accepting the honesty of others is another key characteristic of a higher performing team.

In some families it can be difficult to give open and honest feedback because the family relationship means that family members are concerned about, or even scared of, offending each other. Therefore, when feedback is given it is often taken personally. Unlike a higher performing team, the inner story of a family can remain hidden or repressed rather than open and explicit. That is why it can sometimes make a guest appearance at family gatherings such as weddings and funerals or can unwrap itself when families are cooped up together at Christmas. These are examples of times when people's emotions are likely to be fast and fluid. Inside their minds feelings begin to attach themselves to thoughts that convince the person that now is the time that they must go public and say the honest things they have kept hidden for years. Being entangled by emotions means that how others will react to the level and nature of the honesty is off the agenda. That is until the next day when the person's private self has to deal with the remorse and regret while those who were the recipients of the honesty deal with the rest of the fallout. That is not how honesty works in higher performing teams.

In teams where people claim there is a family dynamic at play, open and honest conversations can be avoided for fear of offending others. Honesty can also be bottled up and expressed at inappropriate times and in an inappropriate way. Honest conversations can be described as "courageous conversations" or "difficult conversations" thus giving some people the opportunity and permission to completely avoid them. When the team knows their inner story and is clear about what it means to be in the team, these conversations are never framed as courageous or difficult, they are seen as respectful, professional conversations aimed at advancing the team's capability to optimise its performance.

'Being' in a team is not the same as 'being' in a family. As a family member I have many years to make meaning about who I am in relation to others and to establish what that means for my developing sense of self. I have time on my side. This will ultimately enable me to become more robust when dealing with challenges that relate to my inner facing and outer facing self. The time factor in a family offers me the opportunity to develop a deeper sense of who I am.

I do not have this type of time luxury in a team. I have to know my self, settle in quickly and relate well to others in the team. This is especially so in competitive contexts where performance conversations are honest, emotional recovery has to be accelerated and where a person's sense of self and identity can be buffeted around on a daily, hourly or even a minute-by-minute basis.

There is an 'I' in Team

I am sure that you will have heard people claiming "There is no 'I' in team". I am not going to go down the route of saying that if you look differently you will see that there is a 'me' and a 'mate' in 'team'. I believe that there is an 'I' in team and there has to be an 'I' in any higher performing team. If you consider previous inner story strands that I have mentioned you will notice that 'my success is your success' shows that there is an 'I' in team. Standing up for your own expertise also places a focus on the 'I' in team, as does the importance of the 'I' in any team where leadership is distributed. Everyone has to serve the team; distributed leadership allows everyone to lead the team too.

In chapter three I explained the difference between being selfish and being self-focused. In a team context, people who are selfish think only about what is best for them. Over the long term selfish people cannot match their own individual ambition with team ambition. Their personal objectives become more important than the team objectives. They will always end up singing their own song. Selfish people can derail and destroy a team and we have to accept that they do exist in some teams. There are times when it can be blatantly evident who the ego-guarding narcissists in a team are as they present as being completely selfish. Interestingly, their narcissism might cause them to give everything when the team is enduring a difficult time because they cannot bear the internal bruising or the external criticism they might personally encounter when things go wrong.

The problem here is that this is not a guaranteed state of affairs. The heightened and alert state of manic vigilance that narcissism can promote might cause them to disengage when times are tough. The actions of other team members can make you vulnerable and there is no recognition or glory available to you when you are associated with a bad performance.

The charming Machiavellians, who are just as destructive to the longevity of team success, can be much harder to spot. They may excel at empathising with other team members but their skill of seeing the world from the standpoint of someone else is a skill that can be flipped and used as a tool for manipulating others. If they know how you see your world and how you make sense of your world they can use that knowledge to manipulate you if they want to. They will end up singing their own song too. If you want to create a higher performing team, narcissists are one type of 'I' in team that you have to be wary of. Those with Machiavellian traits are another 'I' to keep a lookout for.

Self-focused team players know that for the team to reach higher levels of performance and achieve long-term success, their personal goals must dovetail perfectly with team goals. They understand that an individual in a team performs in a collective context and for the greater good of the team. Of course there will be people in teams whose individual spirit may be excitable and irrepressible but if they are a team player it will be harnessed in a way so that the team spirit benefits. Self-focused team members are team players. They have a collective orientation and give everything for the team – but they begin by ensuring that they are clear about their own individual task, how that relates to the task of others and what they are personally committing to do for the team. Their first focus is on the 'I' in team; they begin with self but follow this by looking wider at self in relation to others. In this way their collective orientation ensures that they make the best decisions for the team.

A useful analogy is to imagine a sports team where a player simply thinks about 'me and the ball' when he or she plays for the team. If you have watched young children play ball games this is often the order of the day. As we develop a more mature awareness of self and other, focusing on 'me and the ball' is clearly understood as selfish thinking in a team environment. A self-focused player has the same me-and-the-ball starting point but their focus will expand to whatever else is relevant in helping the team to compete, perform and win. They are also conscious of 'my teammates' and the expansive nature of their thinking does not stop there. They will think about individual members of the opposition, the opposition as a team, the tactical space, the technical space, the physical space and the mental space. In their mind they begin from a self-focused position but are always capable of seeing and understanding the bigger picture. They begin with the 'I' and their thinking expands outwards. This analogy can be applied to multiple teams in multiple contexts.

I have witnessed examples of teams who were struggling to be the best they can be in a competitive environment where both the momentum and outcome of a game changed because of the words of an inspirational leader, captain, coach or team member: the 'I' in team. Superficially all that happened was that someone gathered the team together and said something. But what *really* happened? On a deeper level various types of psychological movement occurred. Minds were altered, commitment was reinvigorated, togetherness galvanised, spirit transformed, resilience fortified and belief in the team's capabilities became renewed and contagious. The result was a winning performance.

The 'I' in team is an important aspect of a higher performing team in other ways too. Individual difference is respected and accepted in higher performing teams and when a person feels connected and respected they are more willing to live the team's inner story. Every individual contributes to identifying barriers and obstacles that will prevent the team from meeting its targets and helps the team to establish what it can do to overcome them. All teams can see the big rocks but higher performing teams can see the small stones too.

The team's inner story should never remain an abstract mystery. It should be known. Knowing your inner story and then changing it when it needs to be changed can and will transform performance.

The Short Story

All teams write and live their inner story.

You can discover and change your team's inner story.

Know what it means to be in the team.

Trust and respect are the lifeblood of team togetherness.

A higher performing team is not a family.

There is an 'I' in team.

Watch out for swashbuckling narcissists and charming Machiavellians.

A team that is high on togetherness can beat a team that is high on talent.

Confidence and belief must not be left unattended.

For higher performance you have to gain clarity about your shared reality.

Chapter Eleven
Understanding Your Changing Story

Now that you have reached the end of this book it may feel like you are at the end of a journey – but this is not the case. When you take a journey into inner space to explore the mysteries of your mind you do not finish by disembarking at a terminus or resting in an arrivals lounge. There is no finishing line or final whistle. There are many other journeys to be taken. It is your mind and there is always something in there that you can explore further and understand better.

After speaking at a conference in Europe I was leaving the conference hall and the organiser was kind enough to thank me for my contribution. Her farewell words were,

"Don't be a stranger."

This was a popular saying within her culture. It was used when someone was about to set off on a journey. The intention was to ensure that I knew that I was welcome to return again. As you are now aware of bounceback it will be obvious to you why I will not be using this phrase when encouraging you to make many return journeys to the inside of your head. Instead, I would like to say,

"Come back soon."

One of the wonders of being human is that we are always learning. No matter who you are or how old you are you are always in a position to learn more. As you make future visits to your mind you will be incrementally more informed about what is going on in there and incrementally more curious. Every visit to the inside of your head provides an opportunity to learn more. You can learn more about why you think what you think, why you feel the way you feel and why you behave the way you do. You can learn more about your self so that you can have the best inner story for you as a professional and as a person. If you stay curious there is always something new to learn.

Thank you for reading *Inner Story*. My intention in writing it was to support you in discovering your inner story and to empower you to make changes where you want to and where you need to. I hope that it has started what will turn out to be a lifelong process for you.

There is still so much more for you to know as you continue to understand your mind and change your world.

NOTES

NOTES

CPSIA information can be obtained
at www.ICGtesting.com
Printed in the USA
LVOW10s0203220217
524936LV00011BA/406/P